Teachers' notes

Introduction

The activities in this book aim to support the implementation of the National Curriculum for English, Attainment Targets 4 and 5, Level 1. They are not designed as teaching tools in themselves but rather they offer children the opportunity to practise newly acquired skills.

In order to gain the maximum benefit from these pages, it is essential that they are incorporated into a learning environment which offers time for talking, listening, thinking, reading and writing. There is always the danger with photocopiable sheets that the children will see them simply as time-fillers or 'colouring activities'. Always explain the purpose of the activity to them so that they concentrate on that aspect of the task.

The aims of this book

The aims of this book are:
• to consolidate knowledge of initial letter sounds with the appropriate letter of the alphabet;
• to provide opportunities to practise letter formation;
• to draw attention to sounds within words, in particular to enable the child to begin to separate the initial letter sound from the rest of the word;
• to enable you to keep a record of initial letter sounds with which the child is familiar;
• to develop the child's control of fine motor skills.

The alphabet letters

Children need to be introduced early in their school life to both letter name and initial letter sound for all the letters of the alphabet. Teaching letter names and sounds isolated from the reason why the child needs to know these skills has been shown to have little effect. It is essential that this skill is used at the appropriate time, for example in consolidating sounds a child has requested in free writing.

These pages take each letter of the alphabet in order. The order in which the letters need to be introduced to the children is up to you. It is generally easier for the child to attach a sound to a letter he can identify by name rather than to name a sound.

Suggested procedure

• Select the letter the children need to practise.
• Photocopy the relevant page.
• Say the name of the letter to the children or ask if they know the name of the letter.
• Ask the children to show you how to draw the letter in the air, using the index finger of the writing hand. Check this for correct letter formation and give help if needed.
• Ask the children to tell you the sound the letter makes.
• Ask the children to point to a picture on the sheet that starts with that sound. Explain that some pictures have been drawn to 'trick' them and that they must choose only the ones that start with the sound of the letter given in the middle of the page.
• Let the children go over the letter in the middle of the page with their fingers. Check again for correct letter formation.
• When the children have achieved this, let them make a 'rainbow' letter by writing the letter outline in four or five colours. Encourage them to try to do this quickly and smoothly.
• Then let the children colour the pictures that start with the letter's sound.
• Ask the children to identify and circle smaller versions of that letter.
• Finally, encourage the children to make a line of letters across the bottom of the page.

Sound check sheets

Pages 26 to 31 comprise five sound check sheets. These offer quick reference for you and the child to see if they can remember the letter sound. The check sheet on page 30 includes letters that some children confuse together. This should only be used when you are certain that the child has a good grasp of all the initial letter sounds. Page 31 is a vowel check sheet.

Initial letter sound record sheet

Page 32 includes pictures for all the letters (except x) ranged around a circular alphabet. You could use this to record letters the child has completed or it could be used as a final check to establish that the child can attach each letter to its initial sound.

Keeping a simple record

A chart similar to the one below could be kept as a simple check sheet for each child in the class.

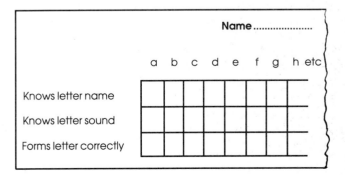

	a	b	c	d	e	f	g	h etc
Knows letter name								
Knows letter sound								
Forms letter correctly								

Name ....

Games and activities

Alliterative sentences

Children delight in tongue twisters and they are an excellent way of drawing attention to initial letter sounds. As the children become more confident they may be able to invent their own sentences or even help you compose some.
• Poor Paul poured porridge in his pocket.
• Gorgeous Gussie gave green gherkins to giggling Gertie.
• Lennie the lion loves licking lollipops.
• Winnie the whale whirls in the wonderful waves.
• Horrible Hattie hates holding hands with handsome Horace.

Guess who?

In this game, you say that you are thinking of someone in the class whose name begins, for example, with 'p' and the children have to guess who it is. An extension of this could be to say that you are thinking of someone whose name starts with the same sound as the beginning sound of 'picture' and 'pocket'.

What will you sell me?

Give each child a letter of the alphabet, then ask them to think of something they would like to sell you that starts with the same sound as their letter. The group takes it in turns to sell you things.

Tracking

This exercise is designed to encourage instant letter recognition. Give each child a piece of text (newspapers and magazines make a useful source) and a crayon or highlighter pen. Explain to the children that they are going to 'track' a letter in the text. Give each child a specific letter and ask them to mark it every time they find it in the text. It is better to tell the child the 'name' of the letter rather than the sound.

Further reading

More detailed discussion about teaching initial letter sounds can be found in *Beginning to Read: Thinking and Learning about Print* MJ Adams (MIT Press, 1990). This gives an overview of research into the place and value of phonics in early reading and writing.

National Curriculum: English

These pages support the following requirements of the National Curriculum for English:

AT4 – Pupils should:
• Write some letter shapes in response to speech sounds and letter names. (1a)

AT5 – Pupils should:
• Begin to form letters with some control over the size, shape and orientation of letters or lines of writing. (1a)

NB The programmes of study for writing, spelling and handwriting are also appropriate.

Scottish 5-14 Curriculum: English language

Attainment outcome	Strand	Attainment target	Level
Reading	Reading for information	Pupils, with teacher support, will find an item of information from an informational text.	A
Writing	Handwriting and presentation	Pupils will be able to form letters legibly.	A

● **Name** _____

My 'a' sheet

1. Write in the big 'a' using four different colours.
2. Colour the pictures of objects that start with the sound 'a'.
3. Find four small 'a's and draw a circle round them.

4. Draw over the line of 'a's, following the arrows.

● **Name** _____

My 'b' sheet

1. Write in the big 'b' using four different colours.
2. Colour the pictures of objects that start with the sound 'b'.
3. Find four small 'b's and draw a circle round them.

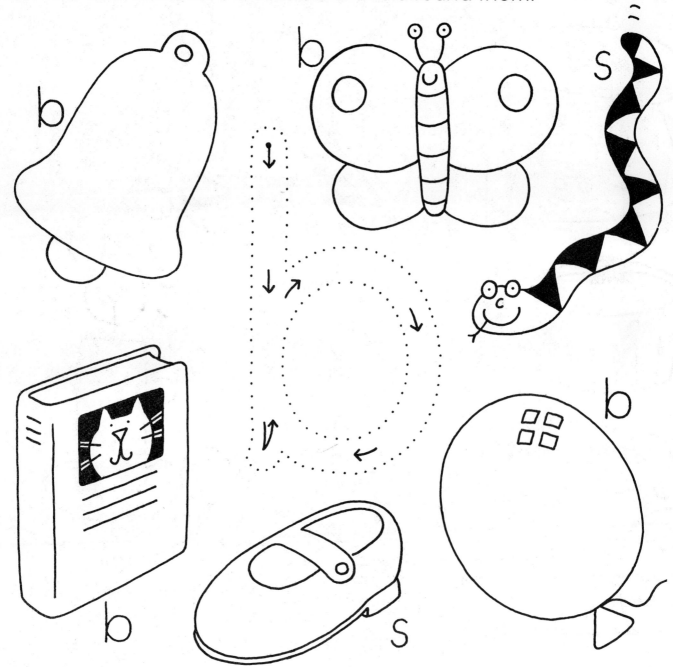

4. Draw over the line of 'b's, following the arrows.

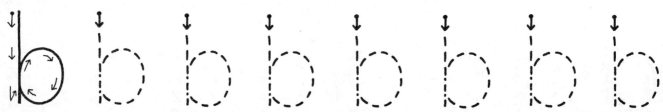

My `C` sheet

1. Write in the big `C` using four different colours.
2. Colour the pictures of objects that start with the sound `C`.
3. Find four small `C`'s and draw a circle round them.

4. Draw over the line of `C`'s, following the arrows.

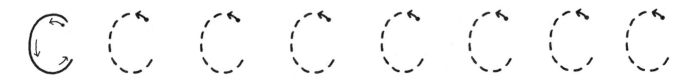

My 'd' sheet

1. Write in the big 'd' using four different colours.
2. Colour the pictures of objects that start with the sound 'd'.
3. Find four small 'd's and draw a circle round them.

4. Draw over the line of 'd's, following the arrows.

My `e´ sheet

1. Write in the big `e´ using four different colours.
2. Colour the pictures of objects that start with the sound `e´.
3. Find four small `e´s and draw a circle round them.

4. Draw over the line of `e´s, following the arrows.

My 'f' sheet

1. Write in the big 'f' using four different colours.
2. Colour the pictures of objects that start with the sound 'f'.
3. Find four small 'f's and draw a circle round them.

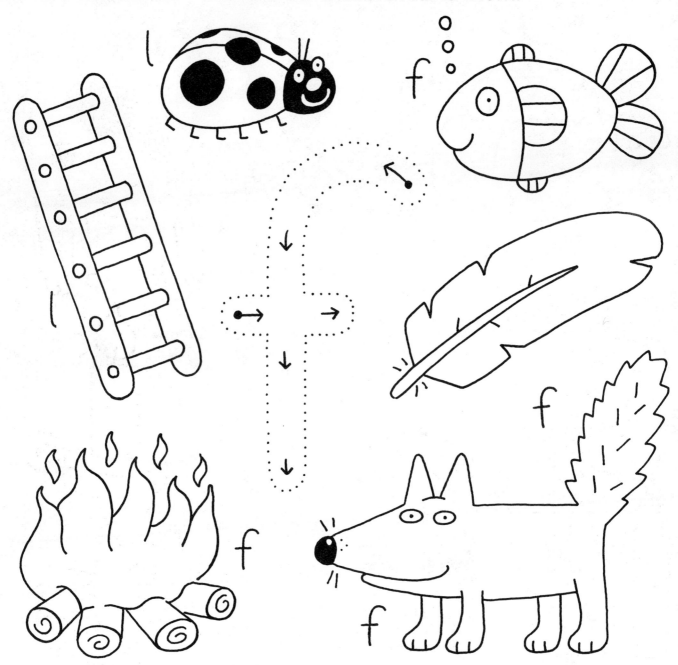

4. Draw over the line of 'f's, following the arrows.

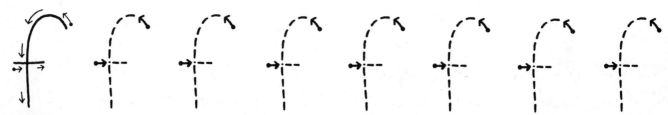

My 'g' sheet

1. Write in the big 'g' using four different colours.
2. Colour the pictures of objects that start with the sound 'g'.
3. Find four small 'g's and draw a circle round them.

4. Draw over the line of 'g's, following the arrows.

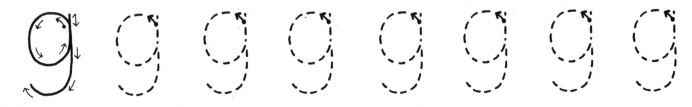

● Name _____

My 'h' sheet

1. Write in the big 'h' using four different colours.
2. Colour the pictures of objects that start with the sound 'h'.
3. Find four small 'h's and draw a circle round them.

4. Draw over the line of 'h's, following the arrows.

● **Name** _____

My 'i' sheet

1. Write in the big 'i' using four different colours.
2. Colour the pictures of objects that start with the sound 'i'.
3. Find four small 'i's and draw a circle round them.

4. Draw over the line of 'i's, following the arrows.

● ESSENTIALS FOR ENGLISH: Initial letter sounds   **11**

My `j´ sheet

1. Write in the big `j´ using four different colours.
2. Colour the pictures of objects that start with the sound `j´.
3. Find four small `j´s and draw a circle round them.

4. Draw over the line of `j´s, following the arrows.

My 'k' sheet

1. Write in the big 'k' using four different colours.
2. Colour the pictures of objects that start with the sound 'k'.
3. Find four small 'k's and draw a circle round them.

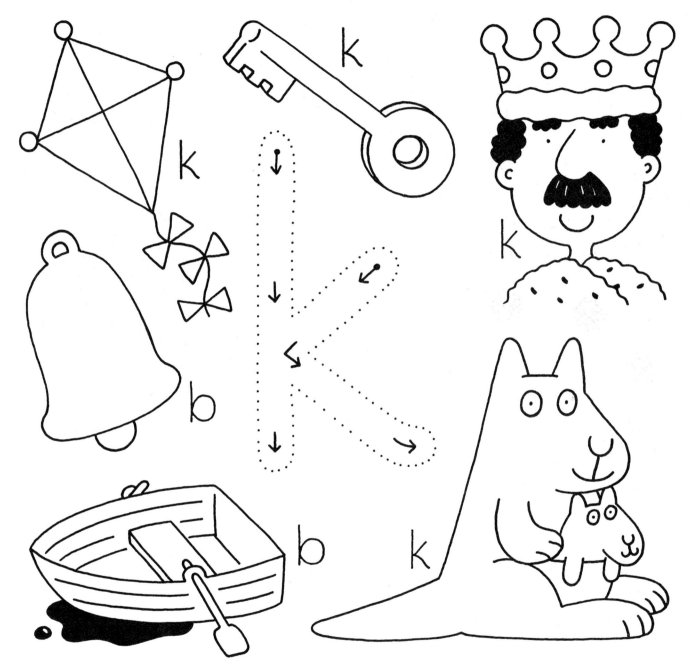

4. Draw over the line of 'k's, following the arrows.

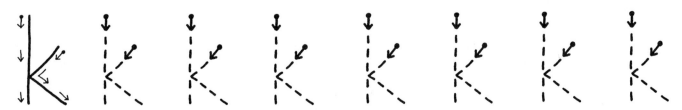

● Name _____

My 'k' sheet

1. Write in the big 'k' using four different colours.
2. Colour the pictures of objects that start with the sound 'k'.
3. Find four small 'k's and draw a circle round them.

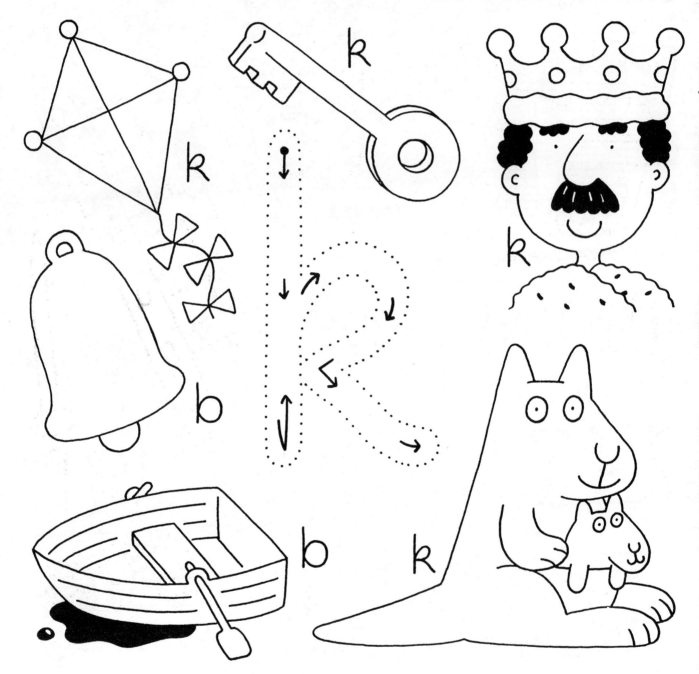

4. Draw over the line of 'k's, following the arrows.

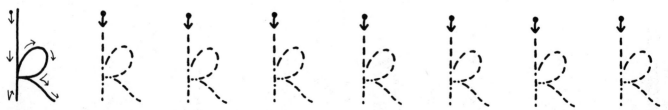

My 'l' sheet

1. Write in the big 'l' using four different colours.
2. Colour the pictures of objects that start with the sound 'l'.
3. Find four small 'l's and draw a circle round them.

4. Draw over the line of 'l's, following the arrows.

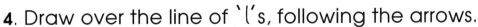

● **Name** _____

My 'm' sheet

1. Write in the big 'm' using four different colours.
2. Colour the pictures of objects that start with the sound 'm'.
3. Find four small 'm's and draw a circle round them.

4. Draw over the line of 'm's, following the arrows.

My 'n' sheet

1. Write in the big 'n' using four different colours.
2. Colour the pictures of objects that start with the sound 'n'.
3. Find four small 'n's and draw a circle round them.

4. Draw over the line of 'n's, following the arrows.

My `O´ and `U´ sheet

1. Write in the big `o´ and `u´ using four different colours.
2. Colour the pictures of objects that start with the sounds `o´ and `u´.
3. Find two small `o´s and `u´s and draw a circle round them.

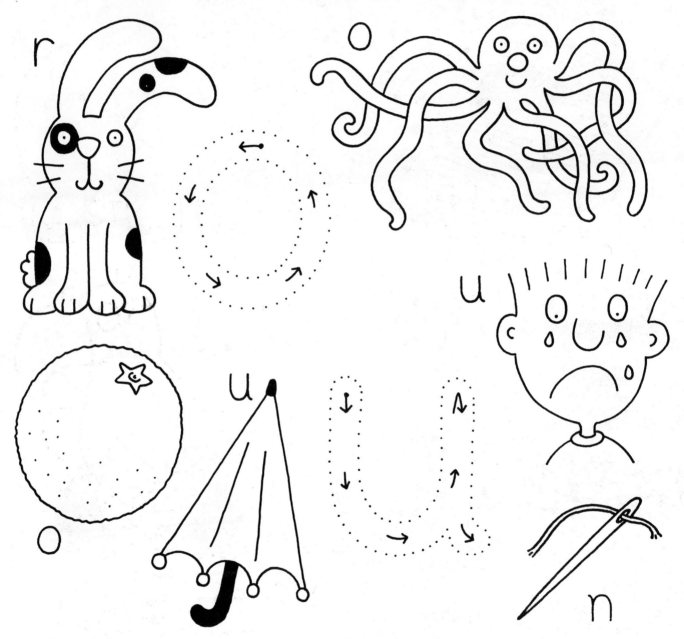

4. Draw over the line of `o´s, and `u´s, following the arrows.

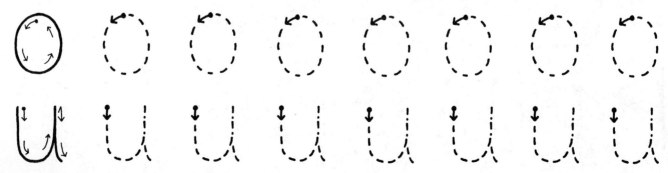

My 'p' sheet

1. Write in the big 'p' using four different colours.
2. Colour the pictures of objects that start with the sound 'p'.
3. Find four small 'p's and draw a circle round them.

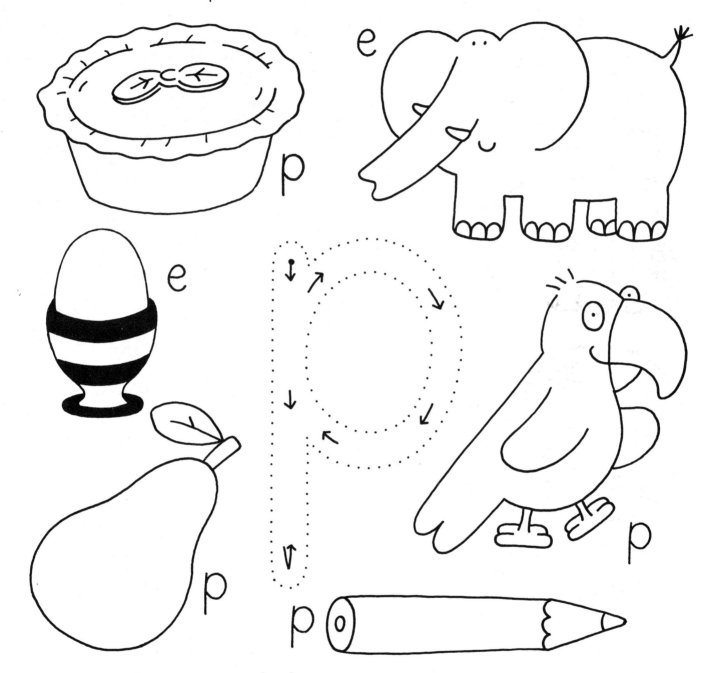

4. Draw over the line of 'p's, following the arrows.

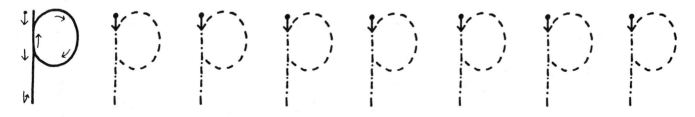

● Name _____

My `q´ and `V´ sheet

1. Write in the big `q´ and `V´ using four different colours.
2. Colour the pictures of objects that start with the sounds `q´ and `V´.
3. Find two small `q´s and `V´s and draw a circle round them.

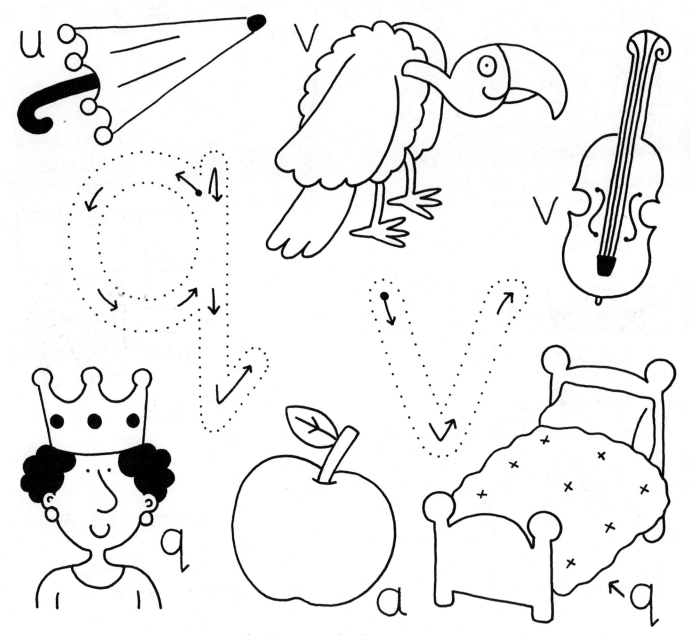

4. Draw over the line of `q´s, and `V´s, following the arrows.

My 'r' sheet

1. Write in the big 'r' using four different colours.
2. Colour the pictures of objects that start with the sound 'r'.
3. Find four small 'r's and draw a circle round them.

4. Draw over the line of 'r's, following the arrows.

● **Name** _____

My 'S' sheet

1. Write in the big 'S' using four different colours.
2. Colour the pictures of objects that start with the sound 'S'.
3. Find four small 's's and draw a circle round them.

4. Draw over the line of 'S's, following the arrows.

● Name _____

My 't' sheet

1. Write in the big 't' using four different colours.
2. Colour the pictures of objects that start with the sound 't'.
3. Find four small 't's and draw a circle round them.

4. Draw over the line of 't's, following the arrows.

● Name _____

My 'W' sheet

1. Write in the big 'w' using four different colours.
2. Colour the pictures of objects that start with the sound 'w'.
3. Find four small 'w's and draw a circle round them.

4. Draw over the line of 'w's, following the arrows.

Name _____

My 'X', 'Y' and 'Z' sheet

1. Write in the big 'X', 'y' and 'z' using four different colours.
2. Colour the pictures of objects that start with the sounds 'X','y' and 'z'.
3. Find two small 'X's, 'y'S and 'z's and draw a circle round them.

4. Draw over the line of 'X's, 'y'S and 'z's, following the arrows.

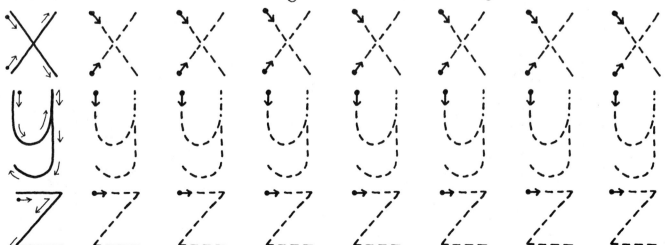

Name _____

My first sound check sheet

1. Colour the pictures of objects that start with the same sound as the picture in the left-hand column.
2. Write the letter by each picture.

b

f

j

k

r

ESSENTIALS FOR ENGLISH: Initial letter sounds 26

My second sound check sheet

1. Colour the pictures of objects that start with the same sound as the picture in the left-hand column.
2. Write the letter by each picture.

My third sound check sheet

1. Colour the pictures of objects that start with the same sound as the picture in the left-hand column.
2. Write the letter by each picture.

Name _____

My fourth sound check sheet

1. Colour the pictures of objects that start with the same sound as the picture in the left-hand column.
2. Write the letter by each picture.

My fifth sound check sheet

1. Colour the pictures of objects that start with the same sound as the picture in the left-hand column.

2. Write the letter by each picture.

● Name _____

My vowel check sheet

1. Colour the pictures of objects that start with the same sound as the picture in the left-hand column.
2. Write the letter by each picture.

● Name _____

Initial letter sound record sheet

Well done!

Contents

Teachers' notes

Introduction

The activities in this book aim to support the implementation of the National Curriculum for English, Attainment Target 2, Levels 1 to 3. They are not designed as teaching tools in themselves but rather they offer children the opportunity to practise newly acquired skills. In order to gain the maximum benefit from these activities, it is essential that they are incorporated into an environment which offers time for talking, listening, thinking, telling, reading and writing.

There is always the danger with photocopiable sheets that children will see them simply as time-fillers or 'colouring activities'. Always explain the purpose of the activity to them so that they concentrate on that aspect of the task.

The aims of this book

The aims of this book are:
• to encourage young readers to sequence logically connected events;
• to become familiar with the conventions of reading sequenced texts in order to adopt this attention to logic into their own writing;
• to offer opportunities to consider different possible endings so that the child comes to recognise that stories have beginnings, developments and conclusions;
• to offer different types of texts for simple sequencing: nursery rhymes, original stories, traditional tales and non-fiction;
• to extend the children's understanding of themselves and the environment in which they live, for example by investigating the seasons, growing up and recycling paper;
• to offer opportunities to work in collaboration with a partner in order to discuss the probable order of events and in this way to clarify their own understanding of causal connections;
• to present children with a variety of texts using a range of grammatical connectives which they should then transfer into their own writing.

The value of teaching story sequencing

Children find it difficult to tell or write a connected narrative successfully. Too often they begin a narrative which is quite obviously not at the real beginning. This is not surprising as children are attracted to the dramatic features of the story and bypass the less interesting albeit necessary scene-setting required by their audience. Similarly, children will forget to follow a narrative through to its logical conclusion and either the end of the story peters out or is extended beyond the attention span of most listeners.

In order to gain confidence and experience, it is best to build upon a child's own sense of sequence acquired through the patterning of well-known rhymes and traditional tales. Even very young children recognise that 'the fox ate up every bit of the little gingerbread boy' is the end of a story. For this reason, the activities in this book include nursery rhymes, traditional tales, well-known stories and Aesop's fables.

As a preparation for sequencing, children should be encouraged to retell stories orally and to recount events that they know or have experienced. In order to keep the child 'on task' and to help her present her story in a logical order, she is likely to need gentle guidance in the retelling through comments and questions. Some older children may benefit from you role-modelling how to retell a simple event, for example, 'Do you remember that we went to look in the school pond? First we put on our coats and then we lined up by the door. Then we crossed the playground....' As a result of this modelling, children will become more aware of the needs of their audience and the vital part that the sequence of events has to play in our lives.

The sequencing activities in this book have been presented in order of difficulty.

Picture sequences

Take time to discuss the contents of the pictures with the children. Encourage them to discuss which picture should be the first before organising the whole sequence. Check that all the children can justify their choice of order. There is no specifically correct order to the events drawn but there is a more likely one.

Ask the children to colour the pictures before they cut them out – once they have been cut out the thin strips of paper are likely to tear if the children try to colour them. The pictures have been kept as simple as possible to help the children keep within the lines when they are colouring.

Pages 5 to 8: Picture sequencing

The content of these four pages has been chosen to reflect situations with which most children will be familiar.
• Wrapping a present
• My lunch box
• Going swimming
• Feeding the cat

Suggestions

Encourage discussion by letting the children work in pairs with a sheet each. Let them colour and cut up the pictures, then put them into sequential order. Then ask the children to tell the story.

Extension activities
• Let the children stick the pictures into their own books or folders.
• Encourage them to add their own text according to their ability.
• Show the children how to make the pictures into a small book, for example using a zig-zag format.
• Stick the pictures on to card and re-use them as a language activity.

Pages 9 to 12: Nursery rhyme sequencing

Some children may find text sequencing easier than pictures. Let the children physically move the sentences around and read them aloud to a friend as this helps them to recognise inconsistencies. These four rhymes have been selected because of their popularity.
• Humpty Dumpty
• Jack and Jill
• Little Jack Horner
• Little Bo-Peep

Suggestions

Make sure that the children are familiar with the selected rhyme. Let them work in pairs with a sheet each to colour the pictures, cut them out and place them in sequential order.

Make a class rhyme book. Ask the children what rhymes they know. Collect these and write them on to the board or a large sheet of paper.

Encourage the children to learn some of the poems by heart. Ask them to join in with you. As they become more confident, see if you can stop and the children carry on with the verse.

Quiz the children on the rhymes that they know, for example, 'What is the line after this one? How does this rhyme end? What comes before this line, eg "And Jill came tumbling after"?'

Extension activities
• Let the children stick the pictures into their own books or folders.
• Encourage them to add their own text according to their ability.
• Show the children how to make the pictures into a small book, for example using a zig-zag format.
• Stick the pictures on to card and re-use them as a language activity.

Pages 13 to 16: What happens next?

These pages offer children the chance to choose from two alternative endings.
• Rags and the cat
• I want some sweets
• Mother hen
• The spaceship

Suggestions

Let the children work in pairs, with a sheet each, and discuss which ending they prefer. When they have chosen an ending, ask them to colour, cut and sequence the drawings as they choose.

Ask the children to consider some situations and decide what they would do. For example, when playing in the garden do you let your baby brother join in or not? When having breakfast who should have the free cereal toy? Who should choose what to watch on the TV?

Extension activity

Let the children offer an alternative ending of their own.

Pages 17 to 20: Picture and text sequencing

These slightly more difficult sequencing activities require the children to read carefully through all the text and to look for clues within the pictures before deciding upon the correct order. The sentences which come first and last are marked to help the order. Many children need to move the strips around physically before coming to a final decision. This activity involves a considerable amount of reading and rereading and can help to consolidate reading for meaning.

These sentences also offer an opportunity to show the children the pointers to be found with sequential texts, eg first..., then..., now....
• Making a go-kart
• Camping
• A trip to the museum
• The wildlife park

Suggestions

Let the children work in pairs with a sheet each. Ask them to read the sentences, cut them up and then discuss and decide on an appropriate sequential order.

Before allowing the children to stick the sentence strips on to a template or page, it is advisable to check the accuracy of their sequencing.

Extension activities

• Ask the children to colour the pictures and stick the sentence strips into their own books or folders.
• Let the children make the sentence strips into an individual book.
• Stick sentence strips on to card and re-use them as a language activity.

Pages 21 to 23: Text sequencing

These three activities all have a science theme and may be usefully linked to classroom work on science.

• The seasons
• Growing up
• Recycling paper

Suggestions

Use the first activity to encourage the children to talk about the seasons and the months of the year.

A way of helping the children to sequence the months correctly is to play 'When is your birthday?' All the children stand in a circle and chant the months of the year. As their month is named any child whose birthday falls in that month ducks down and stays there until 'December' when all the children should be crouching down. On the repeat they stand up as their month is named.

Pages 24 to 27: Well-known tales

It is important to familiarise children with these stories before giving them this activity. This is best done by telling the story in your own words or reading them from a text.
• The hare and the tortoise
• The lion and the mouse
• Cinderella
• Jack and the beanstalk

Suggestions

These sheets require the reader to write a caption text and do a drawing in order to complete the story. Encourage the children to decide what they will write in the space provided before they colour and cut up the page.

Extension activities

• Encourage the children to compare their endings and discuss the different ways they have written the caption texts.
• Let the children write their own version of a well-known story, offering text followed by illustration.

Pages 28 to 29: Modern tales

• Rocky the robot and the spaceship
• Rocky the robot and the supermarket
These two stories provide practice in sequencing sentences. The order of these sentences is not correct on the page. Ask the children to cut them up and then decide the order. When they are happy that the story makes sense, let them stick them into their books.

Pages 29 to 32: Paragraph sequencing

These need to be physically cut up and re-arranged until the child is happy with the sequence. These are suitable for the child who is a confident Level 2 reader.
• The fox and the crow

- The wind and the sun
- The oak tree and the fir tree

Suggestions
The order of these paragraphs is not correct on the page. In order to promote discussion, let the children work in pairs. Encourage them to cut up the page and arrange the paragraphs in the order that they think makes sense. Before pasting it into their books, ask them to read it to a partner.

National Curriculum: English

These pages support the following requirements of the National Curriculum for English.

AT1 – Pupils should:
- describe an event, real or imagined, to the teacher or another pupil. (2b)
- relate real or imaginary events in a connected narrative which conveys meaning to a group of pupils, the teacher or another known adult. (3a)

AT2 – Pupils should:
- describe what has happened in a story and predict what may happen next. (2d)
- listen and respond to stories, poems and other material read aloud, expressing opinions informed by what has been read. (2e)
- read a range of material with some independence, fluency, accuracy and understanding. (2f)
- demonstrate, in talking about stories and poems that they are beginning to use inference, deduction and previous reading experience to find and appreciate meanings beyond the literal. (3d)
- bring to their writing and discussion about stories some understanding of the way stories are structured. (3e)

AT3 – Pupils should:
- structure sequences of real or imagined events coherently in chronological accounts. (2b)
- write stories showing an understanding of the rudiments of story structure by establishing an opening, characters, and one or more events. (2c)
- shape chronological writing, beginning to use a wider range of sentence connectives than 'and' and 'then'. (3b)

Scottish 5-14 Curriculum: English language

Attainment outcome	Strand	Attainment target	Level
Reading	Reading for information	Find, with teacher support, items of information from an informational text.	A
	Reading for enjoyment	Pupils read for enjoyment simple stories supported by pictures.	A
	Reading to reflect on the writer's ideas and craft	Pupils will read and with teacher support, talk about a short, straightforward text showing that they understand one important idea.	A
Writing	Handwriting	Pupils form letters and space words legibly for the most part.	A
	Imaginative writing	Pupils will write a brief imaginative story.	A

Wrapping a present

Colour the pictures. Cut them out and make a story.

My lunch box

Colour the pictures. Cut them out and make a story.

Going swimming

Colour the pictures. Cut them out and make a story.

Feeding the cat

Colour the pictures. Cut them out and make a story.

● Name _____

Humpty Dumpty

Colour the pictures. Cut them out.
Put them in order and make the rhyme.

Humpty Dumpty had a great fall.

Couldn't put Humpty together again.

Humpty Dumpty sat on the wall.

All the king's horses and all the king's men

Jack and Jill

Colour the pictures. Cut them out.
Put them in order and make the rhyme.

To fetch a pail of water.

Jack fell down and broke his crown

Jack and Jill went up the hill

And Jill came tumbling after.

● Name _____

Little Jack Horner

Colour the pictures. Cut them out.
Put them in order and make the rhyme.

He put in his thumb and pulled out a plum

Little Jack Horner sat in the corner

Eating his Christmas pie.

What a good boy am I.

And said, 'What a good boy am I.'

Little Bo-Peep

Colour the pictures. Cut them out.
Put them in order and make the rhyme.

Leave them alone and they'll come home

And doesn't know where to find them.

Bringing their tails behind them.

Little Bo-Peep has lost her sheep

Rags and the cat

What happens next?

Copy the sentences to make the story.
Choose the ending you like best.
Make up the last sentence yourself.

1 _____

2 _____

3 _____

4 _____

I want some sweets

What happens next?

Copy the sentences to make the story.
Choose the ending you like best.
Make up the last sentence yourself.

1 _____

2 _____

3 _____

4 _____

Mother hen

1	2	3
A hen sits on her eggs.	An egg begins to crack.	CRACK!

What happens next?

Copy the sentences to make the story.
Choose the ending you like best.
Make up the last sentence yourself.

1 _____

2 _____

3 _____

4 _____

Name _____

The spaceship

1	2	3
The spaceship is going to the moon.	The spaceman gets out.	He goes down the steps.

What happens next?

Copy the sentences to make the story.
Choose the ending you like best.
Make up the last sentence yourself.

1 _____

2 _____

3 _____

4 _____

Making a go-kart

Read the sentences and cut them out.
Put them in order, then stick them into your book.

They found an old box, some bits of wood, some wheels and some nails.

Tom and Harry were going to make a go-kart. They drew some plans.

Harry pushed the go-kart. Tom turned the steering wheel.

Crash! The go-kart fell to pieces. 'Oh, no!' said Tom and Harry.

It took them a long time to make the go-kart.

At last the go-kart was finished. Tom got in to have a ride.

Camping

Read the sentences and cut them out.
Put them in order, then stick them into your book.

They woke up.
They were very wet.

The children put up a tent
in the garden.

They had supper.
They were having a lovely time.

'Can we sleep in the tent tonight?'
they asked.
'Yes,' said Mum.

They ran into the house.
Mum made them hot drinks.

In the night it started to rain.
It rained and rained.

● Name _____

A trip to the museum

Read the sentences and cut them out.
Put them in order, then stick them into your book.

Lucy jumped with surprise.
The dinosaur winked again
and moved his tail.

Lucy walked into the museum.
She wanted to see the
dinosaurs.

Lucy was going on a school trip
to the museum.

They went to the museum
in a coach.

She looked at the dinosaurs and
one winked at her.

The teacher laughed.
'Don't worry,' he said.
'The models work like robots.'

The wildlife park

Read the sentences and cut them out.
Put them in order, then stick them into your book.

Then they drove to the monkey park.
Peter couldn't see any monkeys.

First they looked at the lions.
Then they looked at the zebras.

Peter was happy.
He was going to the wildlife park
with his family.

'Oh dear, I hope it doesn't rain
on the way home,' said Mum.

They all laughed, but the monkey
ran away with the
windscreen-wiper.

Suddenly a monkey jumped
down from a tree.
He landed on the car.

The seasons

Read the sentences below. Cut them out.
Match the sentences to the pictures.

✂ ------------------------

| In summer the sun feels hot. There is more daylight. We can play outside. | In winter it gets dark early. The weather is cold. We need to keep warm. |

| In spring flowers and trees start to grow. It begins to get warmer. | In autumn, leaves fall from the trees. It begins to get colder. |

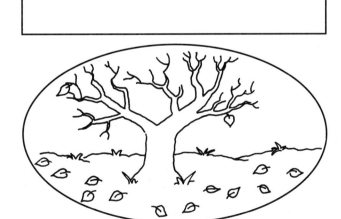

● **Name** _____

Growing up

Read the sentences below. Cut them out.
Match the sentences to the pictures.

✂ - - - - - - - - - - - - - - - - - -
I move slowly and my hair is
going grey. I enjoy seeing my
grandchildren.

- - - - - - - - - - - - - - - - - - - -
I cannot walk or talk yet.
I drink a lot of milk.
I cry when I am hungry.

- - - - - - - - - - - - - - - - - - - -
I can run and jump and I talk
a lot. I can feed myself. I like
playing with my friends.

- - - - - - - - - - - - - - - - - - - -
Now I am grown up I can go
to work.
I can drive a car.

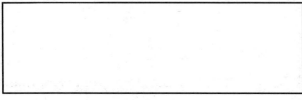

● **Name** _____

Recycling paper

Read the sentences below. Cut them out.
Match the sentences to the pictures.

✂ ------------------------------
We take the bundles to the
lorry. The lorry takes the
paper to the factory.

We can use the paper again
to write our letters.

We save our newspapers.
We tie them into bundles.

At the factory the paper is
recycled.

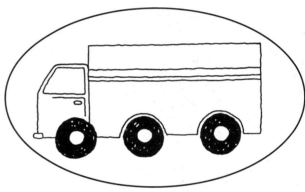

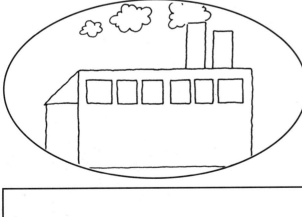

The hare and the tortoise

The ending of the story is missing. Can you finish it?

1
A hare and a
tortoise decided to
have a race.

2

3
The hare had a rest.
He sat down under the
tree and fell fast asleep.

4

Write what happens.

Draw the end of the story.

5

6

The lion and the mouse

The ending of the story is missing. Can you finish it?

2
'I am the strongest animal in the jungle!' said the lion.

4
'I can help you,' said the mouse.
'You are too small to help me,' said the lion.

Draw the end of the story.   Write what happens.

Cinderella

The ending of the story is missing. Can you finish it?

2	
Cinderella couldn't go to the ball. The ugly sisters went without her. Cinderella cried.	

4

Cinderella danced with
the prince at the ball.
She was very happy, but
she had to leave at
midnight.

Draw the end of the story.   Write what happens.

5

6

Name _____

Jack and the beanstalk

The ending of the story is missing. Can you finish it?

2

The next morning Jack
saw a beanstalk growing
into the sky.
He climbed and climbed
to the very top.

4

Jack waited until the
giant was asleep.
He took the hen and
ran off and climbed down
the beanstalk.

Draw the end of the story.   Write what happens.

5

6

Rocky the robot and the spaceship

Cut out the sentences. Put them in order to tell the story.

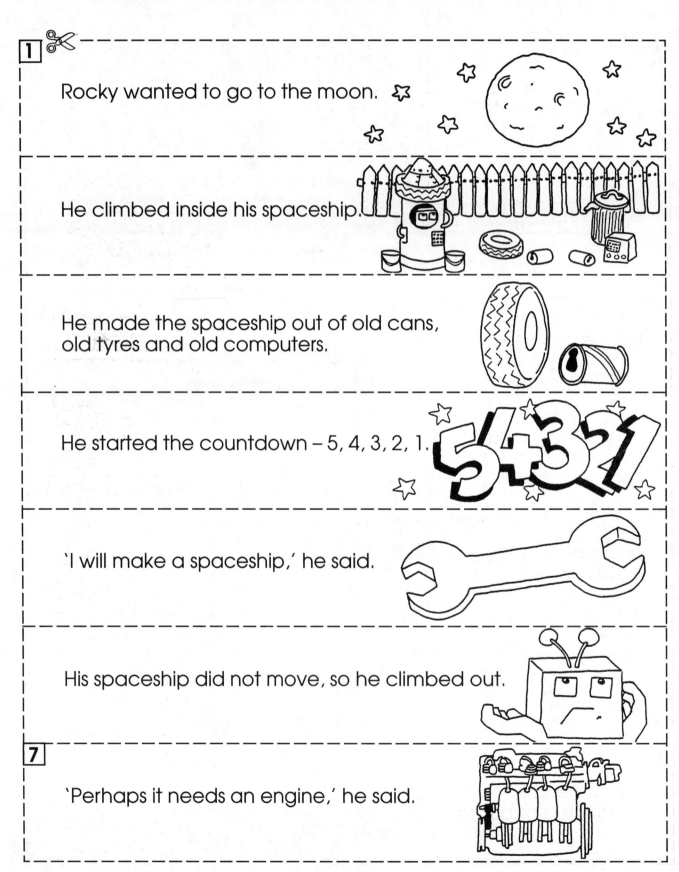

1

Rocky wanted to go to the moon.

He climbed inside his spaceship.

He made the spaceship out of old cans, old tyres and old computers.

He started the countdown – 5, 4, 3, 2, 1.

'I will make a spaceship,' he said.

His spaceship did not move, so he climbed out.

7

'Perhaps it needs an engine,' he said.

Name _____

Rocky the robot and the supermarket

Cut out the sentences. Put them in order to tell the story.

1 Rocky looked in his kitchen.
There was no food left.

He saw the trolleys by the door.
He took one and pushed it into the shop.

Rocky wanted to ride like that
so he got into his trolley.

Rocky saw a little boy sitting
in a trolley.

His trolley rolled into a pile of tins.
The tins fell into his trolley.

'I must go shopping,' said Rocky.
So he went to the supermarket.

7 'That's lucky,' said Rocky.
'I wanted to buy lots of beans.'

The fox and the crow

Colour the pictures. Cut out the paragraphs.
Put them in order to tell the story.

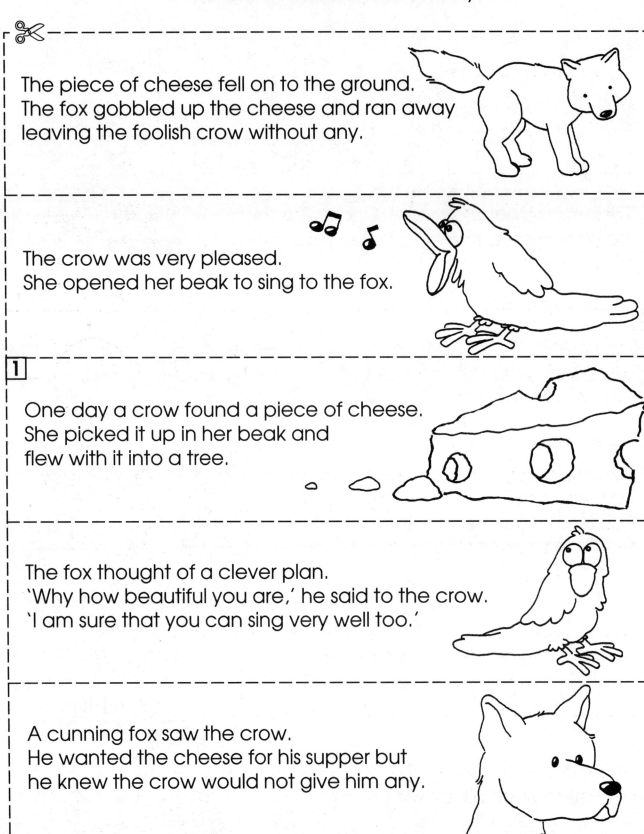

The piece of cheese fell on to the ground.
The fox gobbled up the cheese and ran away
leaving the foolish crow without any.

The crow was very pleased.
She opened her beak to sing to the fox.

1

One day a crow found a piece of cheese.
She picked it up in her beak and
flew with it into a tree.

The fox thought of a clever plan.
'Why how beautiful you are,' he said to the crow.
'I am sure that you can sing very well too.'

A cunning fox saw the crow.
He wanted the cheese for his supper but
he knew the crow would not give him any.

The wind and the sun

Colour the pictures. Cut out the paragraphs.
Put them in order to tell the story.

'Now it is my turn,' said the sun
and he began to shine.
It got hotter and hotter.

The wind saw that the sun had tricked him.
He was so cross that he howled and
blew over the mountains.

1

The wind thought he was stronger than the sun.
'Very well,' said the sun.
'Let us see who is the stronger.'

'I shall be first,' said the wind and
he began to blow.
But the harder he blew the more
the man wrapped his jacket around him.

The sun saw a man walking down the road.
'The one who can make the man
take off his jacket is the stronger,' said the sun.

'This is a very hot day,' said the man
and he took off his jacket.

Name _____

The oak tree and the fir tree

Colour the pictures. Cut out the paragraphs.
Put them in order to tell the story.

That night a terrible storm blew up.
The wind tore through the forest.
The little fir tree bent over with the wind.

1

The oak tree was very proud.
'I am the tallest and strongest tree in the
forest,' he said.
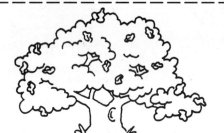

The wind blew against the oak tree.
The oak could not bend and it crashed to
the ground.

He looked down on to the little fir tree.
'How small and weak you are,'
said the oak tree.

The next day the fir tree looked at the
fallen oak tree.
'I may be small and weak,' she said,
'but I know you must bend with the wind.'

'It is true that I am small and weak,'
said the fir tree.
'It is true that you look tall and strong,'
and she waved her branches in the breeze.

● ESSENTIALS FOR ENGLISH: Story sequencing

Contents

Teachers' notes

Aims of this book

The aims of this book are:
• to offer children a range of situations in which to develop confidence as speakers and listeners;
• to give children a variety of opportunities to work with different partners;
• to give scope for important role-playing experience;
• to encourage imagination through play and improvised drama;
• to offer purposeful activities in which to develop pupils' power of concentration, grasp of turn-taking and ability to hold the attention of their listeners;
• to enable pupils to listen and respond to stories and rhymes;
• to prompt them to tell and retell familiar stories.

Developing language skills

Language skills and the ability to communicate effectively underpin success in all curriculum areas. For this reason the National Curriculum places considerable emphasis upon pupils' success in speaking and listening, irrespective of their initial competence or home language. In the busy classroom, it can be difficult for the teacher to ensure that all children have equality of experience through which they can develop as speakers and listeners.

Equality of opportunity

It can happen that some articulate children dominate the 'talk time' in the classroom. This can prevent the more reticent child from making oral contributions. Some children are confident at talking to teachers and other adults, and this may lead the teacher to assume that the same child is as successful a communicator with his or her own peers, which is not always the case. The children who are good at talking to the teacher may find it difficult to grasp turn-taking and the ability to voice disagreement courteously when talking with their peers.

Similarly, some children who are shy at participating in group activities, show through their other school work that, although they may not have spoken very much, they have listened attentively – and this skill is easily overlooked. For this reason, the teacher needs to plan situations and activities which provide equality of opportunity for all children.

The activities in this book focus upon two of the strands within Speaking and Listening identified by the School Examinations and Assessment Council: Responding to literature and Talking with others. Many of the activities require the children to play rhyming games as the ability to recognise rhyme aurally enhances children's ability to read and write.

The structured tasks present the pupils with opportunities to work co-operatively with a partner. It is advisable to keep a record of the partners that children select as otherwise there is a tendency for children to always opt to work with a preferred friend. Whilst this can, on occasions, be a very profitable working arrangement, it may affect the children's range of talking and learning experiences.

The photocopiable activities will prompt purposeful talk and teachers can ensure that all children receive the same encouragement to develop their speaking and listening skills. These activities should also enable the teacher to keep a record of each child's speaking and listening opportunities and performance.

Notes on individual activities

Pages 5-6: Make a mask

These masks, simple to colour and cut out, are an excellent way to encourage children to talk in role. The Programme of Study for Key Stage 1, Attainment Target 1, encourages children to develop their speaking and listening skills through role-play. For this activity four children work together in each group. In order to support children's language in this role-playing activity, it is best to ensure that the children are familiar with the story of Goldilocks and the three bears. The teacher might like to keep the dialogue on task by taking the role of a narrator. Some less confident talkers in the class might benefit from discussing the role before enacting it, e.g., 'What did Daddy Bear say?' 'What did Baby Bear say?'

It is quite possible to extend this role-play fiction-recall activity into a prediction game by asking the children to think what the characters might have said after the end of the story, e.g., 'What did Mummy Bear say after Goldilocks had run off?' Some confident groups of children might like to perform their play for others to watch.

Pages 7-9: Spot the difference

For these activities children work with a partner. First remind the children of the principle of a spot-the-difference activity. They should search for the differences individually and circle each difference as they find it and number it. When both children in each pair have found all the differences they should compare the order in which these differences were found. When they have compared notes they could colour the pictures.
Extension activity: encourage the children to use the pictures to tell one of the well-known tales.

Pages 10-12: What's wrong?

For these activities children work with a partner. They should examine the pictures closely to discover what is wrong in each picture. Before beginning the activity check that the children are familiar with the two nursery rhymes 'Humpty Dumpty' and 'Jack and Jill'. The partners work together to discuss what is wrong in each picture. Encourage the partners to take it in turn to point

out the errors. In this way each child gets an equal opportunity to be involved in the activity.
Extension activity: the children could choose their favourite picture and colour it in.

Pages 13-14: Retelling well-known tales

In these activities well-known tales are depicted in each set of four pictures. Children work with a partner. One child tells the story to his or her partner using the pictures as a prompt. Then the second child tells the story depicted by the second set of pictures. In order to make the most of this oral story-telling it is advisable to ensure that the children are familiar with the plots and also to remind them of the language of well-known tales, e.g., 'Once upon a time...', 'Up and up and up he climbed...', 'Fee, fi, fo, fum, I smell the blood of an Englishman', 'The cruel step-mother...', 'The ugly sisters...', 'Poor Cinderella could not go to the ball...', 'Be sure to return by midnight'. The children could listen to a recording of the relevant fairy-tale as preparation for their own retelling. At the end of the story some children might like to record their retelling.

Pages 15-16: Acting out well-known tales

Through drama and role-play children can gain confidence in oral language. In these activities small groups of children (three to four) can retell amongst themselves the well-known tales. Some children will need to have the tale retold or reread to them before they engage in their own retelling. Once the participants are confident in the retelling they can choose one of the pictures to act out the scene for others to guess.

Page 17: Make an old rhyme

Rhyme is an important acquisition in the developing skills of the young reader. This activity has two well-known rhymes ('Hickory, dickory, dock' and 'Hey diddle diddle') for children to complete. The missing words are in a bank at the end of each rhyme. Each word also has a small illustration, so that even those children who cannot read the words can participate in this rhyming activity. Once the children have filled in the missing rhyming words, encourage them to choose one of the rhymes to learn by heart.

Page 18: Make a new rhyme

This activity is exactly the same as the above, except that the rhyme will not be familiar to the children. Some children may need help from an adult or another child to read the rhyme for the first time, but all should be able to identify the missing words in picture form and then to add them to fill the gaps in the rhyme. Some children might like to learn these rhymes by heart.

Pages 19-20: What will happen next?

For this activity children work with a partner. They take it in turns to describe a picture, i.e., the first child describes picture 1 and the second child describes picture 2. Together they imagine what might be drawn in picture 4. Once they have discussed their suggestions, each child can draw their own ending to the story. It might be very useful to tape-record the children's responses.

Pages 21-22: Make a puppet

For this activity children will need to work in groups of four. Like making masks, using simple puppets gives young children a stimulus for purposeful talk. First ensure that all the children are familiar with the story of the Billy Goats Gruff. Children should then choose a character and colour it in. Those children who are able should be encouraged to cut out on their own their chosen character. Paste the cut-out paper characters on to card and fix a short length of garden cane to the centre of the back of the puppet. The children can then hold on to the cane and use it to move their puppet character.

Page 23: Find the rhyme – 1

For this activity children work with a partner. Each child has a copy of the page in front of them. The first child chooses one of the pictures and puts number 1 in the top right-hand corner. He or she then says the name of the object and the partner must find the word on the page which rhymes with the word they have heard. The partner then puts number 1 in the top right-hand corner of the rhyming word. Then the second child selects a picture and puts number 2 in the top right-hand corner and says the word for the first player, who in turn must find the picture which rhymes with that word. The game continues until all the pictures have been matched with a rhyme. The players then compare their results to see if the matching numbers are indeed rhyming words.

Page 24: Find the rhyme – 2

This activity is played in exactly the same way as Find the rhyme (1).

Page 25: Build a nursery rhyme

The nursery rhyme 'One, two, buckle my shoe', is jumbled up on the page. Children work with a partner to cut out and reassemble the rhyme. Once the rhyme has been put together in the correct order and pasted on to a piece of paper, encourage the children to learn the rhyme by heart with one partner saying the numbers, i.e., 'One, two' and the other saying the verse 'Buckle my shoe'. When they have said the rhyme once, they can swap roles.

Page 26: Rebus rhyme – 1

For this activity children work with a partner to say the rhyme by reading the words and the pictures. Once they can say the rhyme confidently, they can rebuild the rhyme from the jumbled lines on the bottom half of the page. These need to be cut out and then pasted down in the correct order.

Page 27: Rebus rhyme – 2

This activity is exactly the same as Rebus rhyme – 1.
Extension activity: children might like to devise their own rebus version of a nursery rhyme.

Page 28: Choose-your-own fairy story

For this activity children work with a partner. Each child looks at the words and pictures and decides how they would like to invent their own story. When they have decided which pictures they want to use to complete their story, they colour in just those pictures. When they have coloured in one picture per line they can read their own version to their partner. Children may enjoy recording their version on to a cassette.

Page 29: Odd one out – 1

For this activity children work with a partner or with an adult. The adult reads out each line of rhyming words in turn and the child listens for the one which does not rhyme. The child should write the 'odd' word on a separate piece of paper. When all the words have been read the child can check the answers. This game encourages careful listening and for this reason the child should not be spotting the 'odd one out' visually, but *hearing* the difference.

Page 30: Odd one out – 2

This activity is played in exactly the same way as Odd one out – 1.

Page 31: My favourite story

The National Curriculum encourages children to reflect on what they have read. This activity invites children to fill in details of a story they have read. This can then become the basis for discussion about the book and help children to structure their responses. Children should be encouraged to jot down notes rather than write at length, as the page should be a prompt for discussion rather than a writing exercise.

Page 32: A checklist of children's speaking and listening skills

This assessment sheet enables teachers to track carefully a child's developing speaking and listening skills.

National Curriculum: English

These pages support the following requirements of the National Curriculum for English.

AT1 – Pupils should:
• participate as speakers and listeners in group activities, including imaginative play. (1a)
• listen attentively, and respond, to stories and poems. (1b)
• respond appropriately to simple instructions given by a teacher. (1c)
• participate as speakers and listeners in a group engaged in a given task. (2a)
• describe an event, real or imagined, to the teacher or another pupil. (2b)
• listen attentively to stories and poems, and talk about them. (2c)

Scottish 5-14 Curriculum: English language

Attainment outcome	Strand	Attainment target	Level
Listening	Knowledge of language	Knowledge of term 'rhyme'	B
	Listening in groups	Listen and respond by contributing	A
	Listening in order to respond to texts	Listen to a simple story, poem or dramatic text and respond	A
Talking	Talking in groups	Talk to others in a group led by an adult	A
	Talking about texts	Talk about a simple story, poem or dramatic text revealing some reaction to one aspect of it	A

Scottish 5-14 Curriculum: Expressive arts

Attainment outcome	Strand	Target	Level
Expressing feelings, ideas, thoughts and solutions	Communicating and presenting	Participating in play activities e.g., puppets	A
	Creating and designing	As part of play activities, trying to be other people, creatures or objects	A

Make a mask

Name _____

Make a mask

Spot the difference

The Enormous Turnip

● Look carefully at the two pictures. Can you find ten differences?

Spot the difference

The Gingerbread Man

● Look carefully at the two pictures. Can you find ten differences?

Spot the difference

Little Red Riding Hood

● Look carefully at the two pictures. Can you find ten differences?

● **Name** _____

Spot the difference

The Billy Goats Gruff

● Look carefully at the two pictures. Can you find ten differences?

What's wrong?

Humpty Dumpty

● Look carefully at the picture. Can you spot ten things wrong?

What's wrong?

Jack and Jill

● Look carefully at the picture. Can you spot ten things wrong?

Retelling well-known tales

Jack and the Beanstalk

● Look at the four pictures. Tell the story from the pictures and then finish the story on your own.

Retelling well-known tales

Cinderella

● Look at the four pictures. Tell the story from the pictures and then finish the story on your own.

Acting out well-known tales

The Ugly Duckling

● Look at the pictures. Tell each other the story. Act it out for your friends.

Acting out well-known tales

The Little Red Hen

● Look at the four pictures. Act out the story for your friends.

Make an old rhyme

● Put the words in the spaces to make the rhyme.

mouse

Hickory, dickory, dock,
The _____ ran up the clock.
The _____ struck one,
The _____ ran down.
Hickory, dickory, dock.

clock

mouse

● Put the words in the spaces to make the rhyme.

cow

spoon

moon

dog

Hey diddle, diddle,
The _____ and the fiddle,
The _____ jumped over the _____
The little _____ laughed to see such fun
And the dish ran away with the _____

cat

● Now choose a rhyme and learn it.

Make a new rhyme

● Write the words in the spaces.

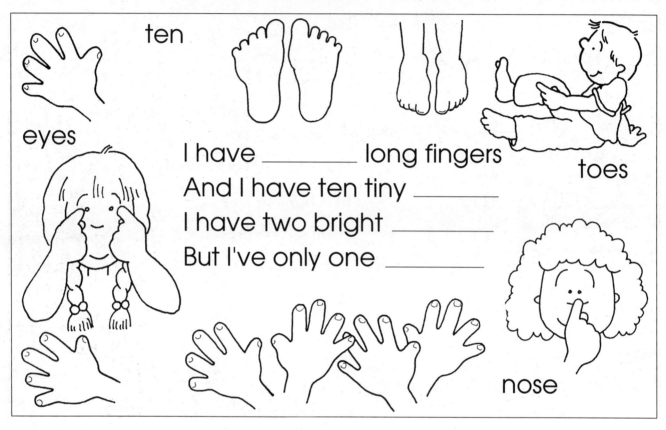

ten

eyes

toes

I have _____ long fingers
And I have ten tiny _____
I have two bright _____
But I've only one _____

nose

● Write the words in the spaces.

mat

I have a pretty little _____
She likes to sit upon a _____
And when I stroke her silky _____
My pretty little _____ will purr.

fur

cat

What will happen next? – 1

● Name _____

What will happen next? – 2

Make a puppet

Make a puppet

Find the rhyme – 1

● Work with a partner. Choose a picture in a square.
  Say the word. Can your partner find the rhyme?

cake

tie

car

rake

eye

star

cat

mouse

tree

rat

house

key

pear

fox

goat

chair

box

coat

Find the rhyme – 2

● Work with a partner. Choose a picture in a square.
Say the word. Can your partner find the rhyme?

bat

flag

frog

hat

bag

log

bell

straw

pen

peg

spoon

duck

egg

moon

truck

shell

door

hen

Build a nursery rhyme

● Can you put the rhyme in the right order? Cut out each part and build the rhyme.

One, two	buckle my shoe.
Five, six	pick up sticks.
Nine, ten	a big, fat hen.
Three, four	knock on the door.
Seven, eight	lay them straight.

● **Name** _____

Rebus rhyme – 1

● Say the rhyme. The pictures will help you.

 sat on a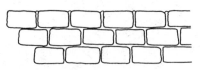

Humpty Dumpty had a great fall.

All the King's

And all the 's men

Couldn't put  together again.

● Now the rhyme is jumbled up. Can you put it in the right order?

All the King's horses

Humpty Dumpty sat on a wall.

Couldn't put Humpty together again.

And all the King's men

Humpty Dumpty had a great fall.

Rebus rhyme – 2

● Say the rhyme. The pictures will help you.

Sat on a

Eating her

Down came a

Which sat down beside her

and frightened   away.

● Can you say this rhyme on your own?
● Now the rhyme is jumbled up. Can you put it in the right order?

| Sat on a tuffet, |
| And frightened Miss Muffet away. |
| Little Miss Muffet |
| Down came a spider |
| Eating her curds and whey. |
| Which sat down beside her |

Choose-your-own fairy story

● Choose the pictures to make the story.

Once upon a time there was a

who lived in a

One day, a

came along who

and the

turned into a

● Now read <u>your</u> story to a friend.

Odd one out – 1

● Read each line to your partner. Mark the odd one out.

not	hot	pot	log
hen	men	set	ten
red	had	bed	fed
met	hit	set	get
did	pin	win	tin
hop	mop	map	top
hid	hip	did	lid
lip	lap	hip	sip
bat	cat	fat	set
cap	pip	map	tap

Odd one out – 2

● Read each line to your partner. Mark the odd one out.

say	day	dog	may
dot	not	top	pot
pit	rip	fit	bit
ran	pan	pen	man
hat	hid	cat	mat
may	met	get	set
bad	dad	did	had
cog	fog	log	let
wet	tin	let	set
win	bin	big	pin

● Name _____

My favourite story

● Fill in the details and then explain your choice to your partners.

Title _____   Saddest part _____

Author _____   _____

Best character _____   Ending _____

Worst character _____   _____

Funniest part _____   _____

_____   _____

● Draw your favourite character here.

A checklist of speaking and listening skills

N.C. Level 1

- ☐ a. Uses talk to enhance play.
- ☐ a. Listens when peers are talking.
- ☐ b. Listens to stories or poems read aloud.
- ☐ b. Indicates response by body language or facial expression.
- ☐ c. Follows single instruction on three occasions.

N.C. Level 2

- ☐ a. Talks in group activities.
- ☐ a. Listens in group activities.
- ☐ b. Describes an event in some detail to teacher.
- ☐ b. Describes an event in some detail to peer.
- ☐ c. Listens with almost complete attention to stories/poems.
- ☐ c. Makes relevant contributions about stories heard.
- ☐ c. Offers suggestions and relates them to stories/poems.
- ☐ d. Asks teacher sensible questions.
- ☐ d. Answers questions with relevant information.
- ☐ e. Follows complex instructions without guidance.
- ☐ e. Gives simple instructions three times.

Comments

_____

_____

_____

Teachers' notes

Aims of this book

These pages of patterns encourage children to practise the motor control of actions and movements which make up our writing system. This is a useful preparation for practising letter shapes. In order for children to practise the patterns further, they could use tracing paper to go over an already completed page or use coloured pencils to go over pencil marks.

The aims of this book are:
- to develop fine motor control;
- to establish a left-to-right directionality;
- to practise the movements necessary in writing;
- to establish the habit of producing small differences between letter strokes, e.g., i/l;
- to allow children to practise making relaxed and comfortable hand movements before having to concentrate on producing specific letter shapes;
- to give children the opportunity to appreciate the differences between 'on the lines', 'above the lines' and 'below the lines'.

Developing handwriting skills

This book contains a series of activities to help children at the initial stage of developing handwriting. It will also be of use to the older children who are not forming their letters properly. Correct formation of letters helps children to achieve a fast and legible hand. There is often a dilemma for teachers when they notice children writing a letter incorrectly, but they are absorbed in their work. Should they stop the child writing and insist upon the correct letter formation, or should they let them finish their writing? Each situation has to be assessed individually, but, on the whole, it is best not to interrupt children who are concentrating on the message they want to communicate. It is better

to wait and then offer a practice page, so that the child learns the correct movement. Children who have become accustomed to incorrect letter formation pose a different problem. They need to spend time re-learning and taking every opportunity to ensure that they finally produce the correct movement without having to think about it.

Posture for writing

- Children should be encouraged to sit well back on the chairs in order to gain maximum stability.
- Children should have their feet firmly on the floor. In a writing corner it may be possible to provide a foot rest (telephone directory) for the smaller child.
- Children should not sit hunched over their writing. This is generally caused by the child being too tall for the chair and table provided. In a writing corner a choice of chairs and table heights could be provided.
- Both hands/arms should be resting on the writing surface. The free hand should be used to control the paper.

Writing implements

- As a rule of thumb, the thicker the barrel of the pencil, the easier it is to produce fine motor control. However, if a pencil is too heavy, then obviously this control is lost. If children are experiencing problems with pencil control, a pencil grip may alleviate the problem. There are a variety of these on the market – some even offer moulded grips which take account of the left-handed, as well as the right-handed child (see LDA and Taskmaster).
- Children do need to experiment with as wide a variety of implements as possible, from wax crayons to felt-tipped pens.

Pen holds

Traditionally, children have been taught to hold the pen between the thumb and the first finger, with the second finger acting as a support. Many children adopt this style very quickly. However, an alternative pen hold has been suggested by Rosemary Sassoon where the pencil is held between the index and the middle finger; this can offer a more comfortable hold and greater pencil control (see *Teaching Handwriting* (1990), Stanley Thornes). Care should be taken to prevent children adopting awkward or tense pencil holds, since this will restrict the speed of their writing as they get older.

Paper position

Young children often prefer to have paper placed directly in front of them, but as they become more confident writers, they should be gently persuaded to move the paper either to the right or left of their body and sloping at approximately 30–40 degrees, according to their handedness. There is no exact position, but comfort and movement across the page should determine the final position.

Helping the left-hander

• Sit the left-handed child on a slightly higher chair so that she can see over the top of the piece of work. This also gives more freedom
of movement.
• If possible, demonstrate letter formation with your left hand.
• A pencil grip can be helpful as left-handers tend to grip very hard. The pencil grip, by thickening the pencil and preventing the fingers from slipping, does relieve some of the pressure.
• Ensure the child has enough space. He should not be knocking either the wall or a friend.
• Encourage the child to try to hold the pencil farther from the point. This enables the left-hander to see what she has written.
• The paper should be positioned to the left of centre and tilted slightly to the right to give more freedom of movement. Young children often find this rather disturbing, and will need gentle but frequent encouragement.

Main handwriting patterns

There are five main handwriting patterns which will be introduced in handwriting families:

1 r n m h p b

2 i u y l t

3 v w x

4 i u y l t (reinforcing pattern)

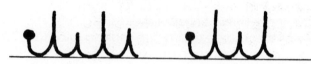

5 a c d e g o q

NB Characters f k j s z are not in a letter family, while some other letters fit into more than one family. It is always worth spending a little time explaining to the children what each activity is trying to achieve in terms of letter formation. Children should not think that handwriting is an easy option, but something which requires hard work and practice, and of which they can be very proud.

Further reading

A Practical Guide to Children's Handwriting, R. Sassoon (1983) Thames and Hudson
The Development of Handwriting Skills: a Resource Book for Teachers, C. Jarman (1979) Basil Blackwell
Handwriting: a New Perspective, R. Sassoon (1990) Stanley Thornes
Teaching Left-handed Children, M. Clark (1974) Hodder and Stoughton
Creating a Handwriting Policy, D. Bentley (1991) University of Reading
Joining the ABC, C. Cripps (1991) LDA

Notes on individual activities

General note: Some children might like to colour the activities using crayons. They should be careful not to obscure the patterns.

Pages 5–6
These two pages introduce to the child the concept of patterns. Encourage him to use the index finger of his writing hand to trace the patterns. This will give him a feel for the rhythm of the pattern and enable the teacher to check on the starting points and left/right sequencing before the child begins with his pencil.

Page 7
This pattern will introduce letters r n m h p b. It is very important that the children start at the dot as this is the starting point. Discuss it with them first, because all letters start at the top, except d and e.

Pages 8–9
These pages offer further reinforcement and practice of the pattern on page 7.

Page 10
This pattern will introduce the following letters: i u y l t.

Pages 11–12
These pages give further reinforcement and practice for the pattern on page 10.

Page 13
This pattern will introduce the letters v w x.

Pages 14–15
These pages offer further reinforcement and practice of the pattern on page 13.

Page 16
This pattern will reinforce the letters i u y l t. The pattern emphasises the ascenders.

Pages 17–18
These pages offer further reinforcement and practice for the pattern on page 16.

Page 19
These patterns will introduce the following letters: a c d e g o q.

Pages 20–21
These pages offer further reinforcement and practice for the pattern on page 19.

Pages 22–23
These pages can be used to check the correct formation of the patterns.

Page 24
Encourage the children to try the patterns by themselves. These can make attractive borders round their work.

Pages 25–30
These pages are for those children whose pencil control needs further reinforcing. The patterns round the edge extend the handwriting patterns.

Pages 31–32
These line guides will provide alternative spacing according to the child's needs and stage of development.

National Curriculum: English

These pages support the following requirements of the National Curriculum for English.

AT5 – Pupils should:
• begin to form letters with some control over the size, shape and orientation of the letters or lines of writing. (SoA, 1a)

• be taught the conventional ways of forming letter shapes, lower case and capitals, through purposeful guided practice in order to foster a comfortable and legible handwriting style. (PoS, KS1, 6)

Scottish 5-14 Curriculum: English language

Attainment outcome	Strand	Attainment target	Level
Writing	Handwriting and presentation	Form letters and space words legibly.	A

Watch points for teachers

Handwriting patterns link up with joined letters.

Tracing patterns and letters can help.

All letters except d and e START AT THE TOP.

Use capital letters at the beginning of words. DO NOT JOIN.

Joined letters help spelling.

Check sitting position. It should be both feet on the floor, forearm on the table.

Wider-lined paper is a help when you are learning to write - or write on every other line.

Encourage children not to hold the pencil close to the point.

Triangular pencils provide a comfortable pencil grip.

Give lots of praise for effort.

If the children like unlined paper, use a line guide.

Name _____

● Follow the pattern with your pencil. Start at the dot.
Practise the pattern in the spaces.

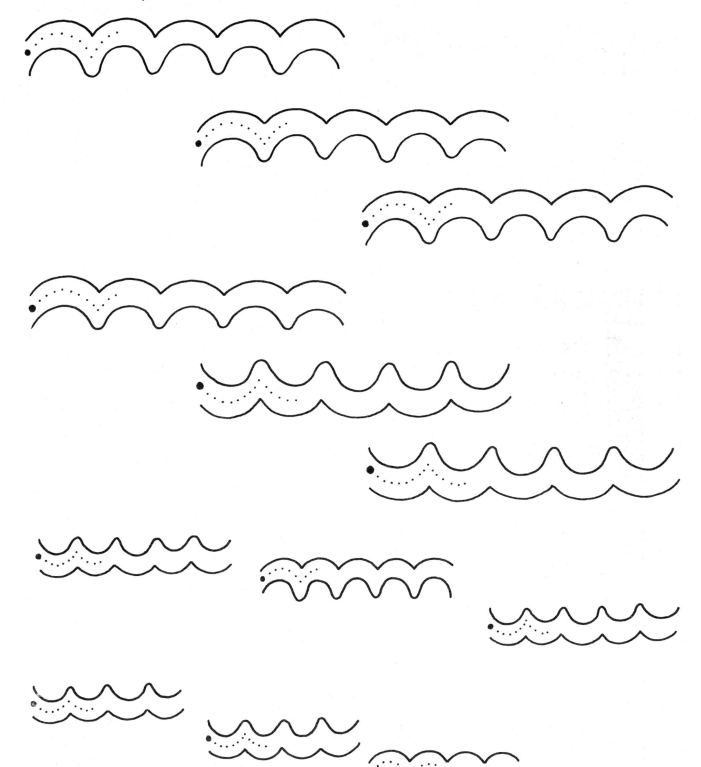

● Try some patterns yourself.

● Follow the pattern with your pencil. Start at the dot.

● Try some patterns yourself.

● Name _____

● Go over the pattern and copy in between. Remember – start at the dot!

m !   mm !   m . !   m . !   m

m .   mm .   m .   m .   m

m .   mm .   m .   m .   n .   m

m .   m .   m .   n .   m .   m .   n

m .   m .   m .   n .   n .   n .   n .   m

● Finish the line.   m n   m n

● Finish the patterns on the fish.

● **Name** _____

● Finish the patterns round the flowers.

● Finish the pattern on the roof.

● Finish the patterns on the tortoises.

● Draw the patterns on the sheep and the birds.

● **Name** _____

● Go over the pattern and copy in between. Remember – start at the dot!

ᘰᘰᘰ ⁝   ᘰᘰᘰᘰ ·   ᘰᘰᘰ ·   ᘰᘰᘰ ·   ᘰᘰᘰ

⁝ᘰᘰᘰ ·   ⁝ᘰᘰᘰ ·   ⁝ᘰᘰᘰ ·   ⁝ᘰᘰ ·   ⁝ᘰ

ᘰᘰᘰ ·   ᘰᘰᘰ ·   ᘰᘰᘰ ·   ᘰᘰᘰ ·   ᘰᘰ

⁝ᘰᘰᘰ ·   ⁝ᘰᘰᘰ ·   ⁝ᘰᘰ ·   ⁝ᘰᘰᘰ ·   ⁝ᘰᘰ

ᘰᘰᘰ ·   ᘰᘰᘰ ·   ᘰᘰ · ᘰᘰ · ᘰᘰ · ᘰᘰ · ᘰᘰ · ᘰᘰᘰᘰ

● Finish the line.   ᘰᘰ ᘰᘰ ᘰᘰ ᘰᘰ

● Finish the patterns on the clowns.

● Finish the patterns on the caterpillars.

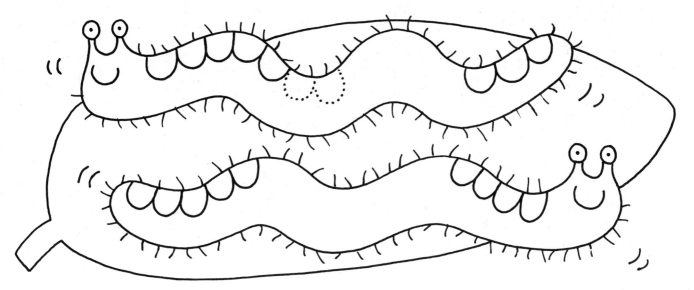

● Finish the patterns on the shells.

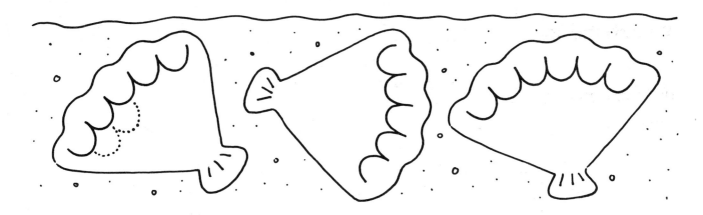

● Finish the patterns on the trees.

● Name _____

● Draw the patterns on the grapes and the flowers.

● Name _____

● Go over the pattern and copy in between. Remember – start at the dot!

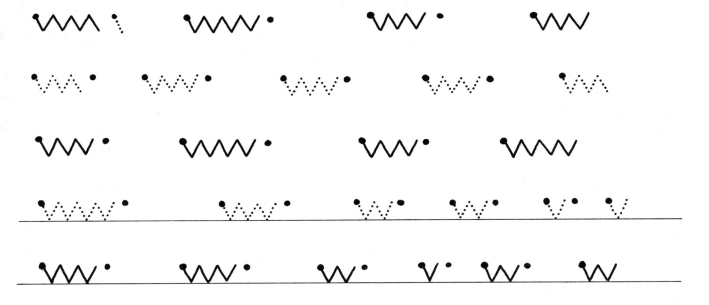

● Finish the line. ___V___W___V___W_____

● Finish the pattern on the dragon.

● Name _____

● Finish the patterns round the suns.

● Finish the patterns on the crowns.

● Finish the patterns on the mats.

● Name _____

● Can you make the clothes look the same?

● Go over the pattern and copy in between. Remember – start at the dot!

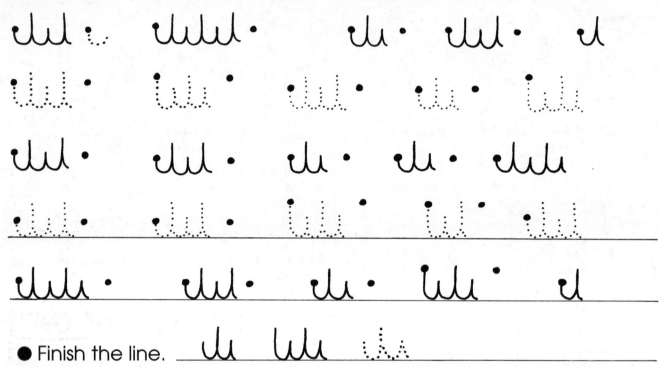

● Finish the line. _____

● Finish the patterns on the balloons.

● **Name** _____

● Finish the patterns on the butterflies.

● Finish the patterns on the socks.

● Finish the patterns on the plates.

● Can you make the books and the hens look the same?

● Go over the pattern and copy in between. Remember – start at the dot!

ccc •   ccc •   ccc •   cc •   cc

ccc   cc •   cccc •   cc •   cc •   •

cc •   cc •   ccc •   cccc •   cc •

cc •   cc •   ccc •   ccc •   ccc •

cc •   cc •   ccc •   cccc •   cc •

Finish the line.   cc cc cc cc _____ .

● Finish the pattern on the owl.

● Name _____

● Finish the patterns on the tiles.

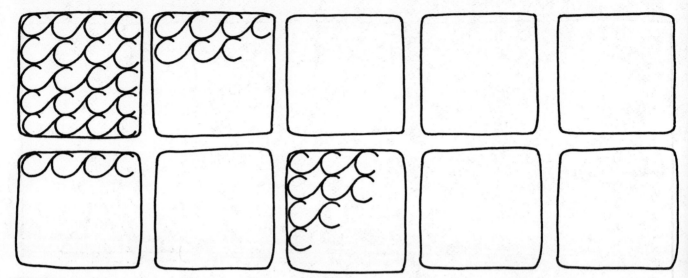

● Finish the patterns on the curtains.

● Finish the pattern on the carpet.

● Can you finish the wave patterns?

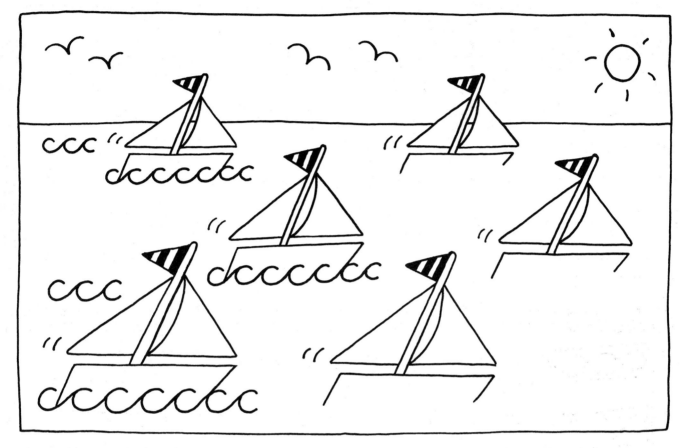

● Go over the pattern and copy in between.

ccc · uuu · cccc · uuu·

ulu · lulul· uuu · mn·

cccc · wwv· wwv· wv·

mn· ulu· m · uuu·

ccc · ccc · ccc · ccc ·

ululul· uuu· mn· uuu·

wwv· wwv· ulu· ulu·

ccccc · ccc · uuu· uu·

mmn· mmn· m· ccc ·

● Now ask a friend to watch you complete the lines.

ccc uuu mn wwv ulu ccc

ccc _____

ccc _____

ccc _____

● Finish each line.

mm mm _____

uuu uuu _____

www www _____

ulu ulu _____

ccc cccc _____

mm mm _____

www ww _____

uu uu _____

cccc ccc _____

ulu ulu _____

● Now ask a friend to watch you complete the lines.
You choose the pattern.

_____

_____

● Can you make up some patterns? Here are some to help you.

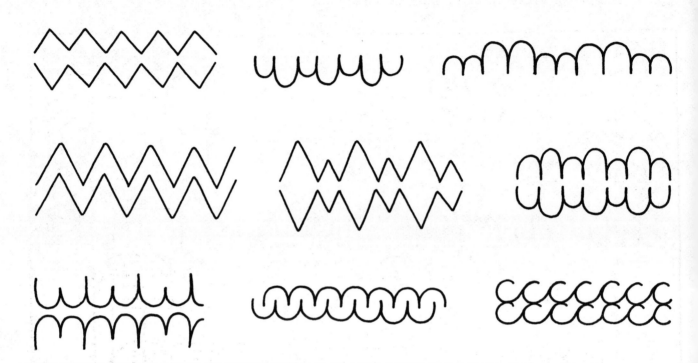

● Draw a pattern in the border.
Now draw a picture inside the border.

Name _____

● Finish the picture and the border. Make the lines and patterns go the same way. Don't use a ruler.

● Finish the picture and the border. Make the lines and patterns go the same way.

Name _____

● Finish the picture and the border. Make the lines and patterns
go the same way. Don't use a ruler.

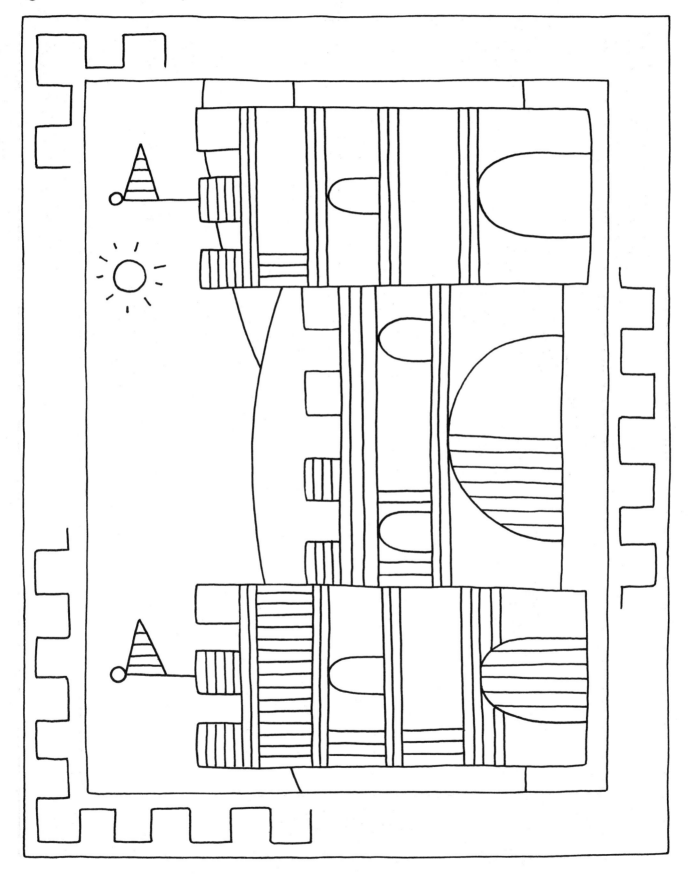

● Name _____

● Finish the picture and the border. Make the lines and patterns go the same way. Don't use a ruler.

Name _____

● Finish the picture and the border. Make the lines and patterns go the same way. Don't use a ruler.

● **Name** _____

● Finish the picture and the border. Make the lines and the patterns go the same way. Don't use a ruler.

Name _____

● Name _____

Contents

Teachers' notes

Introduction

The activities in this book aim to support the implementation of the National Curriculum for English, Attainment Target 3, Levels 1 to 3. They are not designed as teaching tools in themselves but rather they offer children the opportunity to practise newly acquired skills. In order to gain the maximum benefit from these activities, it is essential that they are incorporated into an environment which offers time for talking, listening, thinking, telling, reading and writing.

There is always the danger with photocopiable sheets that children will see them simply as time-fillers or 'colouring activities'. Always explain the purpose of the activity to them so that they concentrate on that aspect of the task.

The aims of this book

The aims of this book are:
• to introduce children to story format;
• to help children at the initial stage of story writing;
• to help children develop into confident story writers;
• to help consolidate the concept of a sentence;
• to provide models of different story styles;
• to familiarise children with ways of presenting characters;
• to familiarise children with ways of developing plot.

Developing story skills

Young writers frequently produce three or four almost unconnected phrases/sentences and proudly announce 'I have written a story'. The role of the teacher is to take the child from this stage into one where the child's writing shows evidence of logical sequenced thought. The best way to prepare children for producing a connected narrative is to build stories orally.

Recount writing

Most children's writing takes the form of recounting something that happened. But this writing often lacks vital information that the audience needs to know in order to make sense of the events. Because the incident happened to the child directly, he or she 'forgets' that anyone who was not present at that particular occasion will need more information if they are to understand the event. This lack of awareness of audience needs is very typical of young children's writing. However, teachers can help by:
• telling very simple reconstructions of familiar events such as 'What we did yesterday', where in a simple oral narrative the teacher recounts the events of the previous day in a logically sequenced order;
• telling a simple reconstruction but this time asking the children to provide missing information, for example, 'Yesterday we went to the fire station. What did we see first? What did we do next?';
• encouraging groups of children to re-build an event with which they are all familiar, keeping

events in chronological order. If a child omits an important piece of information, prompt further reflection by asking such things as, 'Did anything happen after we looked at the fire station and before we sounded the siren?'

Story writing

To invent a completely fictitious story is very difficult for young writers. They need the scaffolding provided for them in the form of suggested settings, characters and plot. The photocopiable sheets in this book provide a variety of story starts to give children the framework for building stories. This should not in any way replace the occasions when a child desires to write entirely what he wants to write. Sometimes children have a very clear idea of the kind of story they want to produce but it is hoped that the practice sheets in this book will give children a better grasp of the elements that build stories. They can then use these same elements in stories of their own creation.

Knowledge about language

Teachers are frequently presented with stories that over-use certain adjectives and depend too heavily on certain connectives – the most familiar of these are the adjective 'nice' and the connective 'and then...'. Teachers can draw attention to the features of language and label the parts of speech when appropriate. This can be introduced when the teacher has read aloud a story. In the ensuing discussion such questions as 'Which words did the author use to describe the giant?' may later be posed as 'Which adjectives did the author use?' This becomes a stepping stone towards children beginning to be aware of the uses of different parts of speech in their own writing. The photocopiable sheets on pages 30 to 32 provide a suggested vocabulary to help children to write their stories and they also encourage children's awareness of the different tools of language. However, simply being able to label the parts of speech is of little value if the child has not also understood the real meaning of this terminology.

Notes on individual activities

Pages 5 to 6: Build a sentence

These activities give children the opportunity to practise building simple sentences. Each sentence has a subject, verb and object. This gives the children a pattern which they can use to construct their own sentences.

Extension activity

Collect vocabulary from the children and write similar sentences on the board.

Pages 7 to 8: Make a sentence

These activities introduce children to having to make a choice of words, but they maintain the tight structure of the sentence so that the children begin to recognise and absorb the main features of the sentence. Children should be encouraged to make both 'sensible' and 'amusing' sentences.

Extension activity

Draw similar columns and ask the children for different nouns, adjectives, verbs and adverbs. Write these on to a large sheet of paper and display them on the classroom wall near the door. The children may like to create their own sentences while lining up for lunch and so on.

Page 9: Choose an ending

Getting children to understand the concept of an ending is one of the most difficult aspects of writing. Children need to be encouraged to consider the way in which they are going to finish a sentence. This activity is best introduced by the teacher talking to the children before they begin to write and providing lots of oral examples for the children to choose from.

Extension activity

Read aloud a variety of endings from different stories. If the children already know the story, encourage them to reflect upon the incidents that led up to the conclusion. If the children do not know the story ask them to guess what might have come before. This reflection helps children to begin to understand that the ending of a story is an integral part of its creation. Children quickly recognise certain traditional endings such as '... and they lived happily ever after', and they can predict the sort of story events that led up to that conclusion – youngest daughter/handsome prince/dragon and so on. The point of the activity is to draw children's attention to the fact that a conclusion ties up all the loose ends of the story. It does not leave the reader puzzled about the fate of certain characters – a feature very common in children's story writing!

Page 10: Choose a beginning

This sheet is slightly more difficult to do than the previous activity. The children need to read through all the choices before they make a final choice. Although all the sentences would work, it is obvious that some make sense while others are improbable. The more confident child could be set the task of creating both sense and nonsense and identifying which sentence belongs to which category.

Extension activity

When reading aloud to children, draw their attention to the different ways authors begin their stories to attract the interest of their readers.

Pages 11 to 12 : Completing stories

These two activities encourage children to think about appropriate speech in different contexts. Suggest to the children that they look through all the sections of text before deciding which extracts of direct speech to fit into each space. This activity presents a useful opportunity to talk with children about how direct speech is presented in written form (in speech marks and on separate lines from the rest of the text). The themes chosen for the activities are ones that should be easily recognised by all children.

Extension activity
Show children how speech is presented in different written forms, for example through comic strips or the combination of speech bubbles and continuous text such as in 'Rupert Bear' stories. It is also worth drawing children's attention to how speech is set out in most story books (with a new line for each character's utterances).

Pages 13 to 14: Build a story

These sentences provide simple story outlines as well as re-enforcing the concept of the sentence. One includes the use of speech marks which have been introduced in sheets 11 to 13.

Extension activity
When the children have completed each sheet they could cut the sentences into strips for another child to reassemble into story order.

Pages 15 to 17: What are they saying?

These three activities are a further development of the earlier direct speech activities. In these activities children are asked to imagine what different characters are saying about a particular situation. This activity is best prepared for by letting children discuss the likely contents of each speech bubble. Ensure that the children understand that they only put the actual words spoken inside each speech bubble.

Extension activity
Let the children look through wordless picture books and decide what different characters might be saying. Remind them to think of words that the character would be likely to use and *not* just the words they themselves might say.

Pages 18 to 19: Identikit pictures

These two activities first provide children with a model for brief descriptive writing and then give them an opportunity to practise that style. Tell the children it is not the quality of the artwork you are interested in, but rather their attention to detail.

Extension activity
Ask the children to work in pairs to write a simple description of someone in the class and see if others can guess who is being described. Remind children that it is only polite to write favourable descriptions of people we know.

Pages 20 to 21: Who am I? What am I?

These two activity sheets provide children with a model for writing short descriptive texts.

Extension activity
Let the children work in pairs to write their own riddles using the model provided. These could be mounted on to card and displayed on the wall for other children to solve. Ask the children to collect riddles and simple jokes and put these into a class book.

Pages 22 to 23: Choose a story

These sheets introduce children to the salient ingredients of a story. Getting children to consider the characters and the setting of their story can help them to structure their stories more clearly. Remember that the author of any story needs to share it with a reader and encourage the children to read their stories to each other.

Extension activity
Let the children provide other sacks of story ingredients for peers. Discuss with them the different openings and story endings that they could use.

Pages 24 to 25: Story prompts

These sheets provide children with a focusing activity to help share their writing. They should work in pairs to discuss the answers to the questions before continuing to write a story on their own.

Extension activity
Encourage the partners to ask more questions and use this procedure to start to consider the beginning, middle and end of each story.

Pages 26 to 27: Tell the story

These two sheets offer children the security of writing a story from pictures. Before they try to do this discuss with them the possible openings they could use and the conclusion they will provide. The stories should not be too long, but they should contain all the actions shown in the pictures. (Children can continue their stories on the back of their sheets.) Encourage the children to edit their retelling so that it is concise and clear rather than a rambling account.

Extension activity
This form of writing is akin to writing for a newspaper. Let the children discuss how they would retell an event for a newspaper and give them an idea of the space and layout that they have to work within.

Pages 28 to 29: Picture story writing

These activities require children to précis their

writing into clear short sentences. Before writing in the spaces provided they need to consider how they will achieve this; which details are essential for the reader and which can be omitted. By providing the space for drawing the pictures on alternative frames the children will also have to consider what details of the plot need to be relayed in the artwork. This should help them to identify the salient points in their writing.

Extension activity

Let the children exchange their stories and talk to their partners about their interpretation of the text and pictures.

Pages 30 to 32: Story borders

These pages not only give children space to create their own stories, but also provide pictorial and vocabulary clues. The vocabulary is divided into nouns, verbs and adjectives to encourage the children to think about these parts of speech when constructing their stories. Some children might like to discuss their story plans with a partner or with an adult helper who should remind them that their stories should have a beginning, middle and an end. When the stories are complete, the children might like to cut off the borders at the top and bottom of the page, leaving the side panels which could be coloured in.

Extension activity

When the children have written their stories, ensure that they are able to share them with the rest of the class/group or partner. Some children might be able to add to the existing table of parts of speech some of the words they have used in their own stories.

The National Curriculum

These pages support the following requirements of the English National Curriculum AT3 Statements of Attainment 1 to 4. Pupils should:

1a. use pictures, symbols or isolated letters, words or phrases to communicate meaning.

2b. structure sequences of real or imagined events coherently in chronolgical accounts.

2c. write stories showing an understanding of the rudiments of story structure by establishing an opening, characters and one or more events.

3a. produce independently pieces of writing using complete sentences, mainly demarcated with capital letters and full stops or question marks.

3c. write more complex stories with detail beyond simple events and with defined endings.

3e. begin to revise and redraft in discussion with the teacher, other adults, or other children in the class, paying attention to meaning and clarity as well as checking for matters such as correct and consistent use of tenses and pronouns.

4b. write stories which have an opening, a setting, characters, a series of events and a resolution and which engage the interest of the reader; produce other kinds of chronologically organised writing.

Scottish 5 –14 Curriculum: English

Attainment outcome	Strand	Attainment targets	Level
Writing	Functional writing	Write briefly for a simple practical purpose.	A
	Personal writing	Write briefly about a practical experience.	A
	Imaginative writing	Write a brief imaginative story.	A

Build a sentence – journeys

● Join the two parts of each sentence. Then write the sentences
on the lines below.

The car went	across the sea.
The ship went	along the path.
The rocket went	down the road.
The bike went	across the field.
The plane went	to the moon.
The tractor went	to the airport.

_____

_____

_____

_____

_____

Build a sentence – animals

● Join the two parts of each sentence. Then write the sentences on the lines below.

The dog	swam in the pond.
The fish	galloped across the field.
The horse	flew into the tree.
The mouse	wagged its tail.
The rabbit	ran into the mouse hole.
The bird	jumped into its hutch.

_____

_____

_____

_____

_____

Make a sentence – 1

● Choose one word from each column to make a sentence, then write the sentences below.

	ugly	mouse	swam		a pond.
The				into	
	pretty	woman	walked		a garden.
	silly	fish	fell		a school.
A	tall	bear	raced	near	a town.
	lucky	robot	skipped		a park.

Here is one example: The lucky robot raced into a school.

1 _____

2 _____

3 _____

4 _____

5 _____

6 _____

7 _____

● Read your best sentence to your friend.

Make a sentence – 2

● Choose one word from each column to make a sentence, then write the sentences below.

The

A

lazy	cat	ran		a house.
			up	
fat	frog	jumped		a tree.
big	man	hopped		a hill.
small	dog	walked	over	a wall.
bad	monster	climbed		a path.

Here is one example: The bad frog climbed up a wall.

1 _____

2 _____

3 _____

4 _____

5 _____

6 _____

7 _____

● Read your funniest sentence to your friend.

Choose an ending

● Choose the ending you like the best and write the sentence on the line.

mashed potato.

I do not like   soap in my eyes.

watching TV.

slug sandwiches.

I like   being tickled.

bouncy castles.

give it to my teacher.

If I had £100 I would   buy lots of sweets.

put it in the bank.

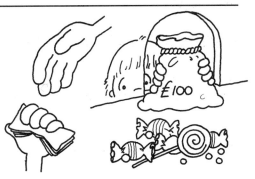

I smile at everyone.

When I am cross   I go cross-eyed.

I look grumpy.

● Read your sentences to a friend.

● Name _____

Choose a beginning

● Choose the beginning you like best and write the sentence on the line.

I get up early

I like to swim   on my holiday.

I come to school

I dig the garden

I watch TV   in my bedroom.

I go to sleep

I go swimming

I put on my shoes   in the bath.

I scrub myself clean

I eat an ice-cream

I pull funny faces   in the car.

I wear a seat-belt

● Read your sentences to a friend.

Completing stories – the picnic

● Sort out the sentences to find out who said what.

'He wants my apple,'   *'Help, help, run as fast as you can!'*

'Let's go for a picnic,'   *'Go away,'*

It was a sunny day.	**1**

_____

said Mum.
We went into a field.

2	A cow came into the field.

_____

shouted Dad.

A horse came into the field.	**3**

_____

said Mum.

4	A bull came into the field. He looked very fierce.

	5

_____

_____

we all shouted.

● Read the story to a friend.

● Name _____

Completing stories – the big puddle

● Sort out the sentences to find out who said what.

'Oh, you naughty boy!'   *'This is fun,'*   *'I went in one little puddle,'*

'Did you go in any puddles?'   *'I will jump in it,'*

Sam saw a big muddy puddle.^{1}
_____

_____

he said.

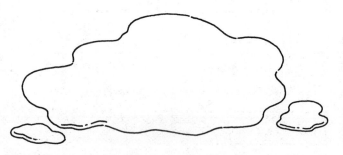

^{2} The water went
over the top of his boots.
_____

he said.

His mum called him in for tea.^{3}
_____

_____

she asked.

^{4} _____

_____

said Sam. But Mum saw that
his socks were very wet.

^{5} _____

_____

said his mum.

● Read the story to a friend.

● **Name** _____

Build a story – my birthday

● Choose the endings for your sentences and write them on the lines.

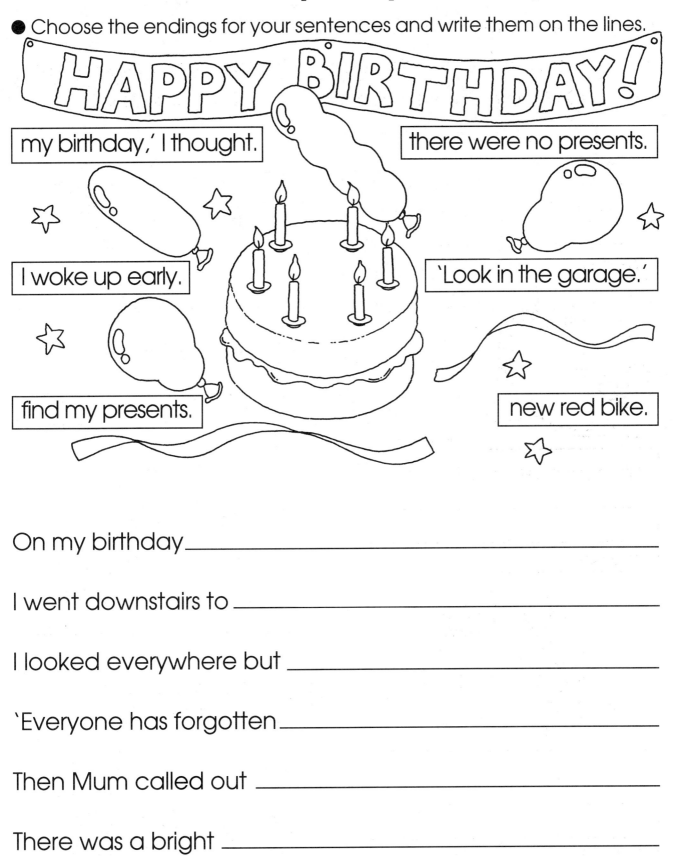

HAPPY BIRTHDAY!

| my birthday,' I thought. | | there were no presents. |

| I woke up early. | | 'Look in the garage.' |

| find my presents. | | new red bike. |

On my birthday _____

I went downstairs to _____

I looked everywhere but _____

'Everyone has forgotten _____

Then Mum called out _____

There was a bright _____

● Read your story to a friend.

Build a story – the little chicks

● Choose the endings for your sentences and write them on the lines.

| three tiny chicks. |
| laid three brown eggs. |
| to keep the eggs warm. |
| No. |
| Yes. |
| so was the hen. |

One day a hen _____

She sat on her nest _____

Were the eggs ready to hatch after ten days? _____

Were the eggs ready to hatch after twenty days? _____

Out of the eggs came _____

The farmer was pleased and _____

● Read your story to a friend.

Watching television –
what are they saying?

● Look at the picture. What is everyone saying? Write their words in the speech bubbles.

The aliens have landed –
what are they saying?

● Look at the picture. What is everyone saying? Write their words in the speech bubbles.

The traffic jam –
what are they saying?

● Look at the picture. What is everyone saying? Write their words in the speech bubbles.

Identikit pictures – 1

● Read the descriptions, then draw the characters.

Sneaky Sue

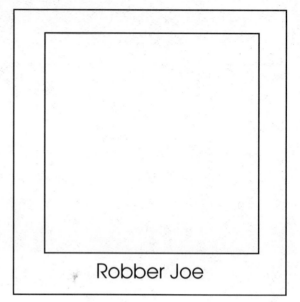

Robber Joe

She has long hair.
She wears glasses.
Her ears stick out.
She has crooked teeth.

He wears a black patch.
He has a scar below his lip.
He has no front teeth.
His hair is black.

● Look at the pictures, then choose their names and write their descriptions.

_____   _____

_____   _____

Identikit pictures – 2

● Read the descriptions, then draw the characters.

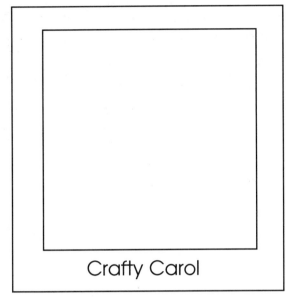

Crafty Carol

Nick-it Nick

She has short black hair.
She wears fancy glasses.
She has a nasty smile.
She has rosy cheeks.

He has a moustache.
He has an unshaven chin.
He wears a baseball cap.
He has a crooked nose.

● Look at the pictures, then choose their names and write their descriptions.

_____   _____

_____   _____

Who am I?

● Read the riddles and write the answers.

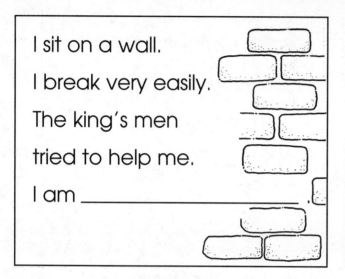

I sit on a wall.

I break very easily.

The king's men

tried to help me.

I am _____ .

I went up a hill.

I carried a bucket.

My brother fell down

the hill.

I am _____ .

I have two ugly sisters.

I went to a ball.

I lost a slipper.

I am _____ .

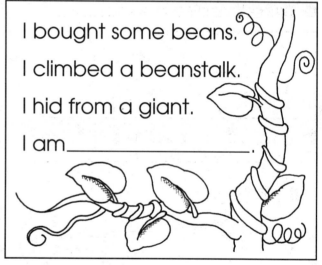

I bought some beans.

I climbed a beanstalk.

I hid from a giant.

I am _____ .

● Write three sentences for your own riddles..

_____

_____

_____

I am little Red Riding-hood.

_____

_____

_____

I am Snow White.

● Now make up some more.

What am I?

● Read the riddles and write the answers.

I grow on a tree.

You can eat me.

I have pips and a core.

I am an _____

I have four wheels.

You can drive me.

I plough the fields.

I am a _____

● Write three sentences for your own riddles.

_____

_____

_____

I am a chair.

_____

_____

_____

I am a clock.

_____

_____

_____

I am a bird.

_____

_____

_____

I am a book.

● Now make up some more.

Choose a story – 1

● Choose one item from each sack. Decide how your story goes.
Write your story on the lines.

Character	Setting	Plot	Ending

a giant
a teacher
an alien

castle
classroom
space ship

gets lost
discovers gold
catches a thief

makes friends
appears on TV
goes on holiday

Title _____

Once upon a time _____

_____

_____

_____

_____

_____

_____

_____

_____

● Read your story to a friend.

Choose a story – 2

● Choose one item from each sack. Decide how your story goes.
Write your story on the lines.

Character **Setting** **Plot** **Ending**

a tiger
a mouse
a donkey

a cave
the jungle
a field

runs away
drinks a magic potion
is caught in a trap

changes into a frog
finds a new home
rescued by a friend

Title _____

Once upon a time _____

_____

_____

_____

_____

_____

_____

_____

_____

● Read your story to a friend.

Story prompt – the monster

● Read the questions and talk over your answers with a friend, then write your own story. Remember to give it a title.

- Imagine you meet a monster.
- What is its name?
- What does it look like?
- What does it like to eat?
- What do you do?

Title _____

_____

_____

_____

_____

_____

_____

_____

_____

Story prompt – the holiday

● Read the questions and talk over your answers with a friend, then write your own story. Remember to give it a title.

- Imagine you can have a holiday anywhere.
- Where would you go?
- What would you take?
- Who would you go with?
- What would you do?

Title _____

_____

_____

_____

_____

_____

_____

_____

_____

● Name _____

Tell the story – the bank robbery

● Write the story shown in the pictures. Give your story a title.

Title _____

_____

_____

_____

_____

_____

_____

Tell the story – the rescue

● Write the story shown in the pictures. Finish the story and give your story a title.

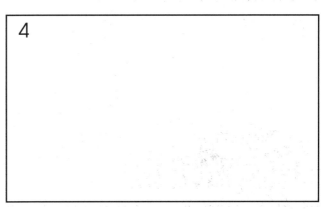

Title _____

_____

_____

_____

_____

_____

_____

Picture story writing – the castle

● Draw the missing pictures and write the missing text, then finish the story.

1

One day two children decided

to explore an old castle. They

walked up the crumbling steps to

the massive wooden door.

2

_____

_____

_____

_____

3

They decided to open the chest

and they went towards it. At that

moment they heard the heavy

door of the room slam shut.

4

_____

_____

_____

_____

Picture story writing – the caves

● Draw the missing pictures and write the missing text. Now finish the story.

1	2

One sunny day the children wanted to have a picnic. Mum said, 'You can go to the beach but do not go in the caves.'	_____ _____ _____ _____

3	4
The cave was dark and damp and not interesting at all. They turned to leave when they saw water lapping around their feet. The tide was coming in!	_____ _____ _____ _____ _____

A deep-sea adventure

● Use the pictures and words in the boxes to help you write your story.

Nouns		Verbs		Adjectives	
ship	treasure	sank	explore	large	angry
squid	diver	attack	found	dangerous	rusty
portholes	mast	swam	rescue	silent	frightening
barnacles	sand	return	search	broken	rotten

Name _____

A dragon in the playground

● Use the pictures and words in the boxes to help you write your story.

Nouns		Verbs		Adjectives	
fire	teachers	scared	feed	friendly	gentle
scales	teeth	breathing	rode	lonely	hungry
smoke	nostrils	running	moving	surprised	heavy
school	tail	laughed	patted	enormous	angry

Lost on a desert island

● Use the pictures and words in the boxes to help you to write your story.

Nouns		Verbs		Adjectives	
danger	waves	built	despaired	lonely	rough
signal	canoe	sheltered	swam	frightened	large
footprints	sand	fished	rescued	hungry	strange
coconuts	rocks	lapping	cooked	isolated	happy

Contents

Teachers' notes

Introduction

The activities in this book aim to develop and support children's non-chronological writing skills. Writing in forms other than narrative is a requirement of the English National Curriculum AT3, Levels 2 to 4.

These activities are not designed as teaching tools in themselves but rather they offer children the opportunity to practise newly acquired skills. In order that the children gain the maximum benefit from these activities, it is essential that they are incorporated into an environment which offers time for talking, listening, thinking, telling, reading and writing.

There is always the danger with photocopiable sheets that children will see them simply as time-fillers or 'colouring activities'. Always explain the purpose of the activity to them so that they concentrate on that aspect of the task.

The aims of this book

The aims of this book are:
• to introduce children to the different purposes of writing;
• to offer examples of the different forms non-chronological writing can take;
• to consolidate the teacher's instructions for non-narrative writing;

• to provide practice of the different kinds of texts required;
• to provide models of different conventions found in non-chronological writing.

The development of writing

It has been recognised that children progress through easily identifiable stages when developing as writers. Each child will vary as to the length of time they remain within each stage; some children may progress very quickly through the early stages of writing when they first come to school, some may even have already moved to the phonetic or transitional stage before they reach school, while others may have very little understanding of the link between marks on a page and the message they wish to convey.

The 'scribble' or pre-communicative stage

The importance of this first stage of writing has only recently been recognised. When children make marks on paper and then proudly declare that they have written 'your shopping list' or even ask an adult what they have written – they are demonstrating that they already have considerable knowledge about writing. They know that the marks on a page represent a message, that this is written on to paper and that it should then be read by someone else. Frequently, the 'scribble' moves from left to right across the page and sometimes gaps are left to represent the spaces between words.

The semi-phonetic stage

Children move from the pre-communicative stage into one where they are making the first steps towards linking the sounds of words to letter shapes. This generally comes through the recognition of their name and then moves on to such things as linking the name of their local supermarket with a specific letter, or pointing towards the letter 'M' and saying 'that says McDonalds'. Their scribble will probably now contain many letter shapes or letter-like shapes.

During this stage they will also consolidate their knowledge of the left to right convention and begin to leave spaces between the 'words'. They will begin to use letters to represent whole words or syllables, for example, 'R' for 'are', or 'wL' for 'whale'. In other words, they will 'hear' the name of the letter within the word and use that letter to represent the sound.

Without the skilled eye looking at this writing it can appear to be indecipherable, but careful examination often discloses that some of these writers have also understood the consistency of language. They may not know how to write in the conventional form but they do know that words stay the same each time they are written. One child in this stage who was very fond of jokes wrote 'I sA I sA I sA' (I say, I say, I say). This important step shows that the child has made the link between letters and words and now needs to be taught how to represent them in a more conventional form.

The phonetic stage

As children become immersed in the rich print environment of school they are likely to have their attention continually drawn to words for both reading and writing. They will begin to be able to distinguish the initial sounds of words from the rest of the word and may frequently write words with the vowels missing, for example 'dg' for 'dog', 'mnstr' for 'monster'.

During this stage children need to learn the sounds that letters make and be able to accurately attach that sound to the letter. This can be achieved by offering plenty of practice through rhyming or through playing games which require the child to concentrate on initial letter sounds, blends or digraphs.

However, also during this stage many children will begin to write some words correctly. They will have developed a 'written sight vocabulary' of frequently used words such as here, is, my, but. As they become more proficient writers they gain

a larger 'written sight' vocabulary, but when they need to write an unusual word they usually revert back to the pure 'phonic' stage and represent that word in the way in which it sounds to them.

The transitional stage

Many children progress very quickly through the previous three stages but the transitional stage between the phonic writer and the correct writer may take up to seven years of schooling. Here the writer is expected to rely far less on how a word 'sounds' and instead to aim to reproduce how a word 'looks'.

The work of Margaret Peters showed that if children want to become accurate and proficient spellers then eventually they will come to recognise how a word looks rather than hope to tackle it phonetically. The teacher needs to train children to look at words and memorise the visual pattern. Peters suggested that children should *look* at the word; *cover* the word; *write* the word; and *check* the word. If this approach is adopted, the children can see when a word does not 'look right', and either have another attempt or consult a dictionary or teacher. In this way they gradually become accurate spellers of all words, even those that did not follow a phonic pattern.

The correct stage

Children of any age may be at this stage. Very young children may not have an extensive vocabulary, but if they have mastered all the words they want to write then they could claim to be 'correct' spellers. These children need to have their vocabulary extended and should be offered activities that do this rather than spending time on spelling lists of words that they are unlikely to use in their writing. These children already know how to learn to spell a word, now they need to become so fascinated by words that their written vocabulary increases.

Notes on individual activities

Pages 5 to 8: making lists

Before these activity sheets are used, the children need to discuss various lists already familiar to them. Find out if they can respond to such questions as 'Why do we write lists?', 'How do lists help us?' and 'How do we write them?' Also, collect together the children's own ideas for different kinds of lists, such as presents lists, shopping lists, and lists of names and addresses.

Extension activities

The children can be encouraged to write lists when using the play shop or home corner, such as shopping lists and jobs to be done. Lists can also be written of each the children's favourite things, such as colours or toys.

Ultimately, their findings can be used to compile frequency tables, bar charts and simple block graphs.

Pages 9 to 12: labelling

These activity sheets provide labelled models from which the children are able to use the same labels to label different pictures. Although the pictures are of the same subject, they are not an exact replica. This ensures that the children transfer their knowledge rather than just copy from one sheet to another. Some of the sheets also include additional labels to be written. Before doing these activities, the children will need to be shown the conventions of labelling, such as writing from the left.

Extension activities

The children can work in pairs, one drawing an object for the other to label. The roles can then be changed over. Encourage them to discuss any labelling that might have been omitted.

Pages 13 to 14: notices and environmental print

These activity sheets enable the children to appreciate the necessity of notices, signs and instructions within the environment. Initial discussions about the signs and labels which the children can see in the classroom and around the school will be helpful. You could also draw their attention to the use of capital letters for this type of writing.

Extension activities

The children can be encouraged to write their own notices and signs for the various areas in the classroom or school.

Pages 15 to 18: writing postcards and addresses

This activity introduces children to the conventions of writing both a postcard and an address.

Before giving the sheets to them, ask them to bring in postcards from home. Explain to them the way postcards are divided into two sections, one for writing a brief message, the other for writing the correct address.

Extension activity

Blank postcards could be given to the children so they can write to their friends. A postbox can also be set up in the classroom.

Pages 19 to 21: finding out from charts

These activity sheets require the children to interpret a simple chart and to convert this knowledge into succinct informative sentences.

Extension activities

Provide the children with a blank outline sheet with a similar format to these charts. Ask them to work in pairs and devise their own chart on any subject of particular interest to them. Encourage them to use information books.

Pages 22 to 23: writing charts from text

These two activity sheets offer the reverse activity to the previous one. The children have to read the text and convert the information into a simple chart. Encourage them to find out further facts from books.

Pages 24 to 26: writing from grid references

These activity sheets provide the children with the opportunity to interpret and record from grid references. A preliminary discussion will be needed on how to use grid references if the children are not familiar with them.

Extension activities

The children can work in pairs drawing up their own maps of islands or routes to school.

Pages 27 to 28: recipes

Recipes follow a specific formula. Children need to be able to write clear instructions which others can follow. These activity sheets provide simple models so that the children can become familiar with this format. This can be adapted if necessary to reinforce simple recording for science investigations and experiments.

Extension activity

Display a collection of various recipes.

Pages 29 to 32: reporting

Children can find it difficult to organise a report of an incident into a logical sequence. These activity sheets provide the framework to enable them to assimilate this format. It can be beneficial for the children to work in pairs to promote discussion and any similarities or differences can be noted.

Extension activity

Encourage the children to devise their own incidents and to dramatise them, for example 'the lost shoes', 'the missing lunchbox' and 'the torn book'. Reports can be written after participating in the drama session.

National Curriculum: English

These pages support the following requirements of the National Curriculum for English:

AT3 – Pupils should be able to:
- structure sequences of real or imagined events coherently in chronological accounts. (2b)
- produce simple, coherent non-chronological writing. (2d)
- shape chronological writing, beginning to use a wider range of sentence connectives than 'and' and 'then'. (3b)
- produce a range of types of non-chronological writing. (3d)

Scottish 5-14 Curriculum: English language

Attainment outcome	Strand	Attainment target	Level
Writing	Functional writing	Write briefly for a simple practical purpose	A
	Imaginative writing	Write a brief imaginative story	A

Scottish 5-14 Curriculum: Mathematics

Attainment outcome	Strand	Attainment target	Level
Shape, position and movement	Position and movement	Use grid references to read or plot location on a grid	B
Information handling	Organise	By entering data in a table using row and column headings	B

● Name _____

A party list

Katie and Ranjit are having a party.
● Help them with their shopping list by choosing six things they will need.

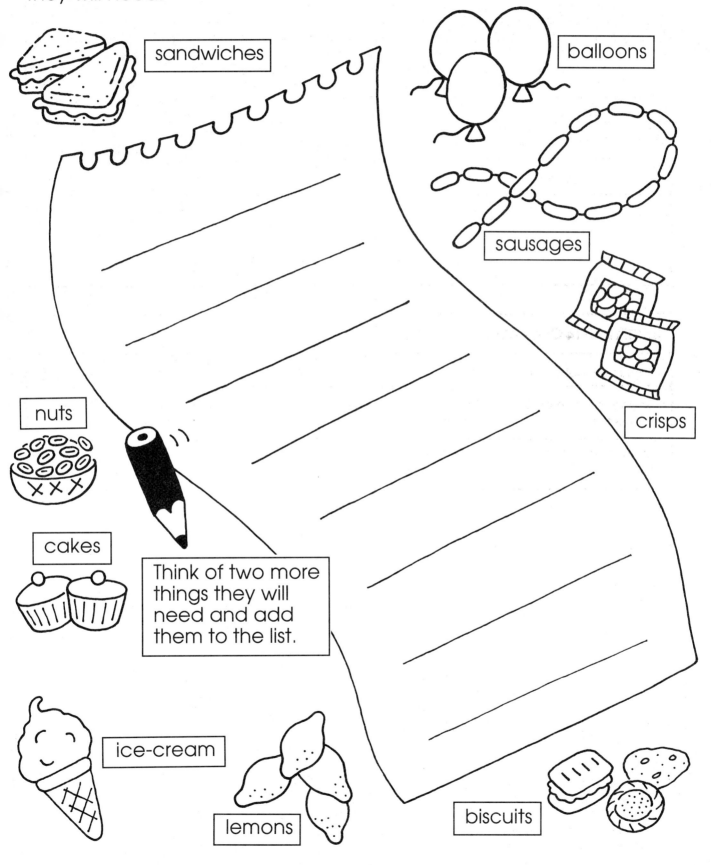

sandwiches

balloons

sausages

crisps

nuts

cakes

Think of two more
things they will
need and add
them to the list.

ice-cream

lemons

biscuits

● Name _____

The giant's list

The giant is going to cook his dinner.
● Help him to buy six things. He is very hungry.

8 loaves of bread

1 pair of monster glove

5 cartons of eggs

9 sacks of potatoe

70 pies

3 books

Think of two more things he will need and add them to the list.

4 sacks of apples

6 packets of rice

40 tubes of toothpaste

2 dustbins of lemonade

The spaceman's list

The spaceman is going on a journey.
● Help him to pack. Choose six things he will need.

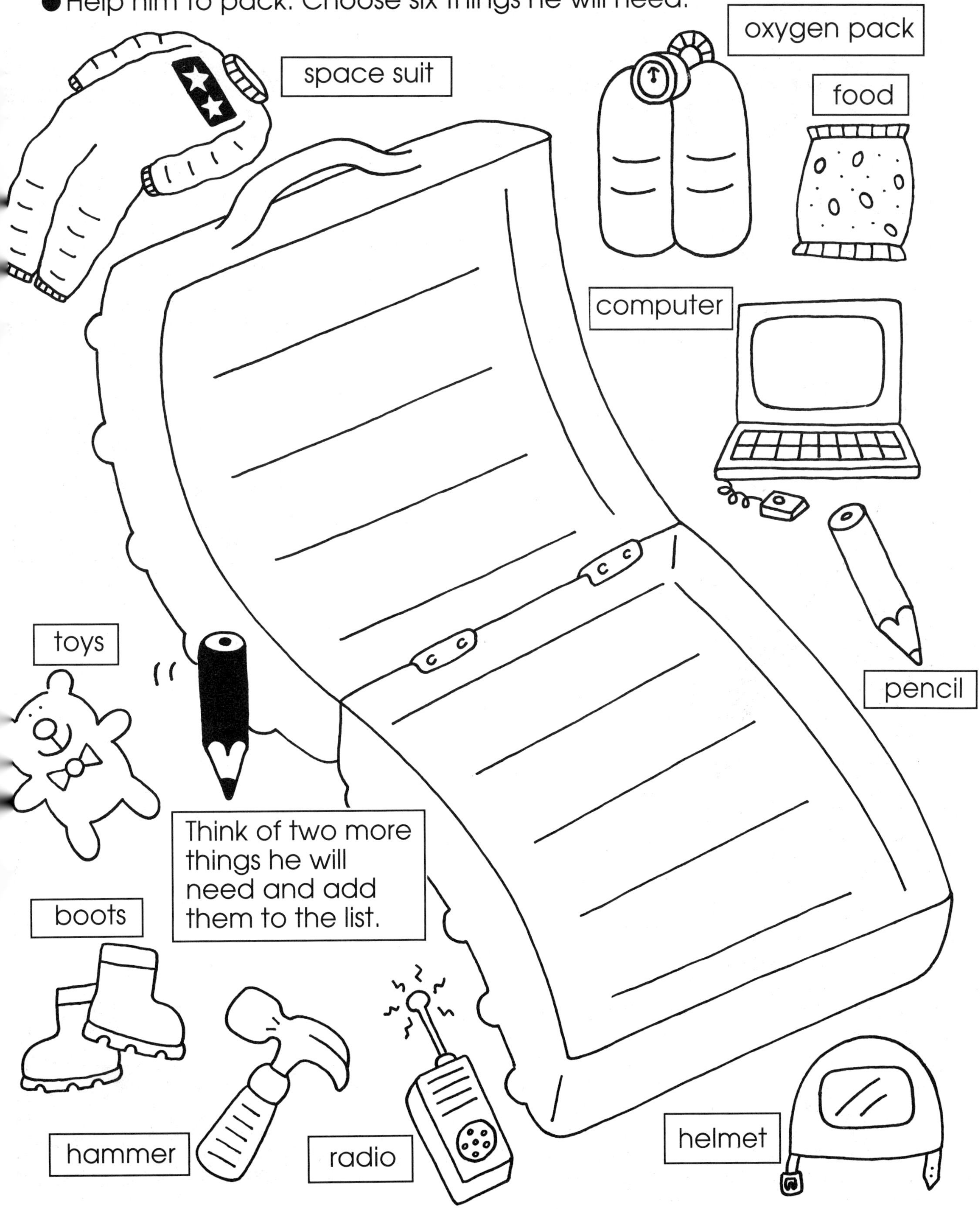

oxygen pack

space suit

food

computer

toys

pencil

Think of two more things he will need and add them to the list.

boots

hammer

radio

helmet

The footballer's bag

The footballer has an important match to play.
● Choose six things to put in his bag.

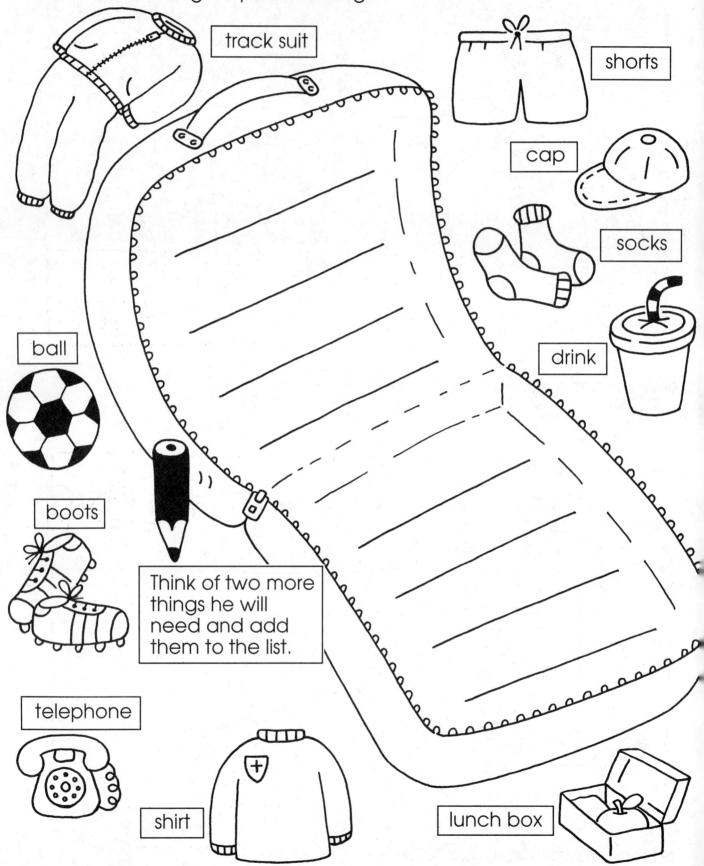

track suit

shorts

cap

socks

ball

drink

boots

Think of two more things he will need and add them to the list.

telephone

shirt

lunch box

Do you know the parts of the body?

head

neck

body

arm

foot

leg

● Write in the names of the parts of this person.

● Now label his knees and hands.

Do you know the parts of the face?

● Write in the names of the parts of this face.

● Now label his cheeks and his lips.

Name _____

Do you know the parts of a flower?

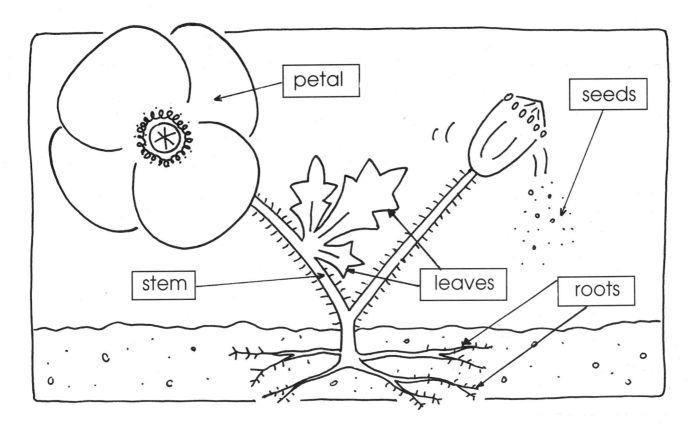

petal

seeds

stem

leaves

roots

● Write in the names of the parts of this flower.

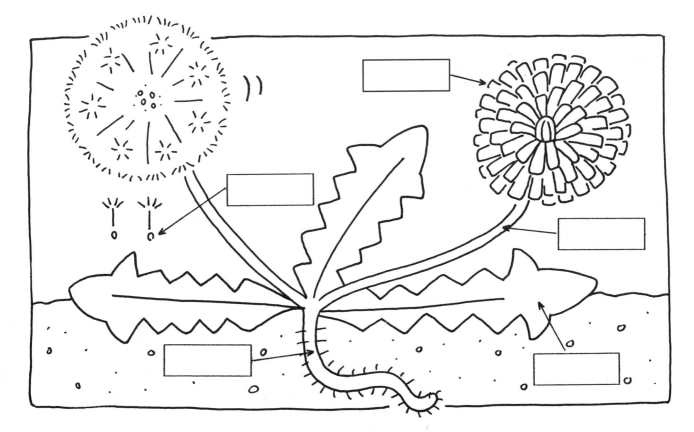

● Name _____

Do you know the parts of a bicycle?

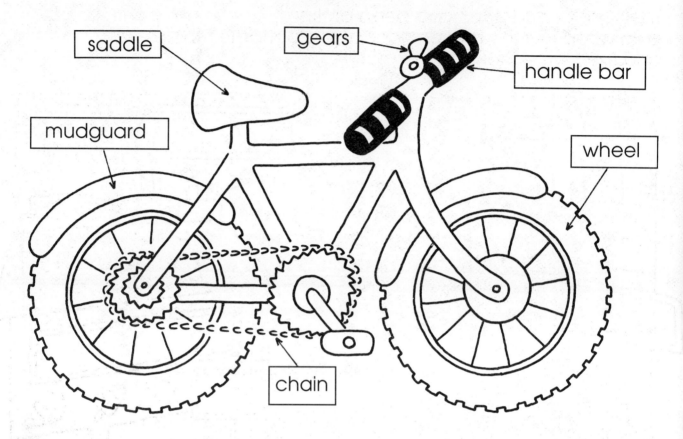

saddle gears handle bar mudguard wheel chain

● Name the parts of this bicycle.

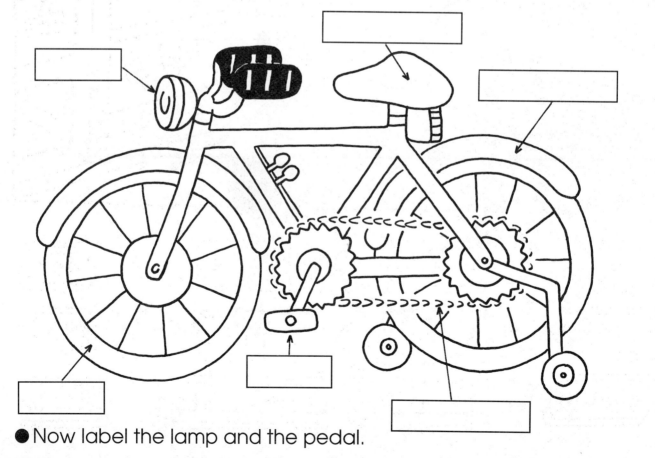

● Now label the lamp and the pedal.

At the shopping centre

The signs in this town have been broken.
● Put together the broken signs at the bottom of the sheet and then write them on the picture.

park phone News box

Car papers Tele To

cream Ice the toilets Post

● Name _____

At the park

The signs in the park have been broken.
● Put together the broken signs at the bottom of the sheet
and then write them on the picture.

● Name _____

A postcard from the seaside

● Finish the picture of the seaside and colour it in carefully.

● Finish writing this postcard and send it to someone you know.
Ask your teacher to help you with the address.

Dear _____

   We are having a

_____ time at the

seaside. We go to

the_____ every day.

We play _____

_____

_____ .

Love from_____

Address

_____

_____

_____

_____

● Name _____

A postcard from a caravan site

● Finish the picture of the caravan site and colour it in carefully.

● Finish writing this postcard and send it to someone you know.
Ask your teacher to help you with the address.

Dear _____

   This is a _____ of
our caravan site. There
are lots of _____ to
play with. We can see
many _____ on
the river. _____
_____.
Love from _____

Address

_____

_____

_____

_____

_____

● **Name** _____

A postcard from a castle

● Finish the picture of the castle and colour it carefully.

● Finish writing this postcard and send it to someone you know.

Dear _____

   I am enjoying

the school _____ to

the castle. We went

down into the _____.

They were dark and

_____

_____ .

Love from _____

Address _____

_____

_____

_____

_____

A postcard from a fun park

● Finish the picture of the fun park and colour it in carefully.

● Finish writing this postcard and send it to someone you know.

Dear _____

  I am having a
great time. I went
on a _____ slide and
got wet. The little
train went _____

_____

_____ .

Love from _____

Address

_____

_____

_____

_____

Finding out from charts – 1

● Read this chart carefully. Write about the horse and the rabbit.

	size	colour	food	habitat	number of legs
a horse	big	brown or black or grey	grass hay oats	field stable	four
a rabbit	small	brown or white or black	grass carrots lettuces	field hutch	four

A horse

_____

_____

_____

_____

_____

_____

A rabbit

_____

_____

_____

_____

_____

● Look at books about them and see what else you can find out.

● Name _____

Finding out from charts – 2

● Read this chart carefully. Write about the goldfish and the robin.

	size	colour	food	habitat	number of legs
a goldfish	small	orange red	flies insects fish food	pond or tank	none
a robin	small	brown and red	worms nuts bread	gardens nest	two

A goldfish

_____

_____

_____

_____

_____

_____

A robin

_____

_____

_____

_____

_____

● Look at books about them and see what else you can find out.

Name _____

Finding out from charts – 3

● Read this chart carefully. Write about the spider and the butterfly.

	size	colour	food	habitat	number of legs
a spider	small	black or brown or white	flies	web	eight
a butterfly	small	many colours	leaves	plants	six

A spider

_____

_____

_____

_____

_____

_____

A butterfly

_____

_____

_____

_____

_____

_____

● Look at books about them and see what else you can find out.

Writing charts from text – 1

● Read the descriptions of the dog and the cat and fill in the chart at the bottom of the sheet.

The dog has short brown fur and a tail. He is small with pointed ears. He has a red collar and his name is Sam. He likes to sleep in his basket by the window. But he barks loudly when the postman comes down the path.

The cat has long grey fur and a long fluffy tail. She has bright blue eyes and pointed ears. She likes to sleep in a box under the table. She purrs happily when the sun shines. Her name is Sukey. She is a very friendly cat.

	name	colour	sleeping place	sounds	shape of ears
the dog					
the cat					

● Write about a cat or dog you know.

Writing charts from text – 2

● Read the descriptions of the elephant and tiger and fill in the chart at the bottom of the sheet.

An elephant is a very large animal. He lives on the plains and he eats leaves and plants. He has a grey wrinkly skin and he uses his trunk to reach up high and pick leaves. A baby elephant is called a calf.

A tiger is a large wild cat and he lives in jungles. He has a striped coat and he eats meat. He can move very quickly on his four legs. A baby tiger is called a cub.

	size	type of skin	food	habitat	name of baby
an elephant					
a tiger					

● Find out something else about a tiger or elephant.

ESSENTIALS FOR ENGLISH: Writing for a purpose   23

Writing from grid references – 1

● Look at this pirates' treasure map.

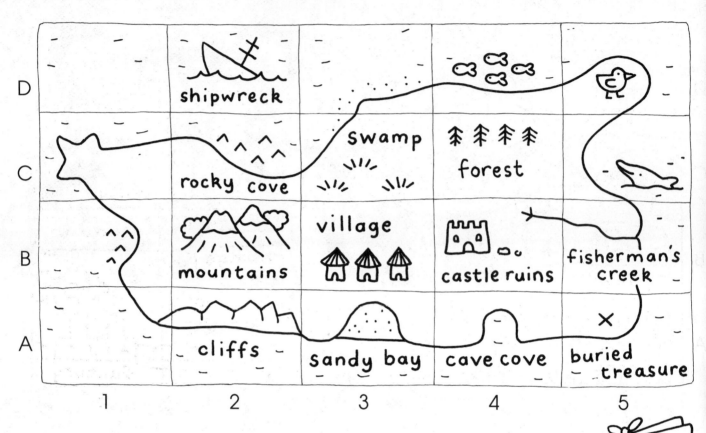

● What did the pirates find at the following grid references?

2C _____   3A _____

3B _____   2D _____

● Which way did they go to find the treasure?

The pirates landed at Rocky Cove 2C and walked past the swamps at

3C. Then _____

_____

_____

_____

_____

Writing from grid references – 2

● Look at this street map.

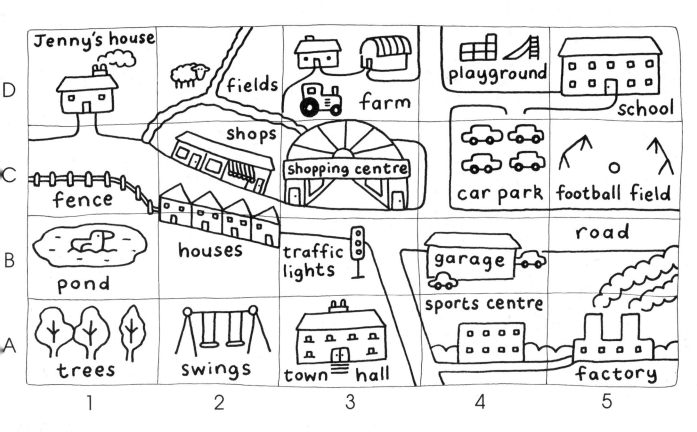

● Jenny lives in a house at 1D. What does she pass on her way to school?

1B _____   3C _____

2C _____   4C _____

● Jenny's dad works at the factory at 5A. He collects Jenny from school and then goes home. Which way does he go?

Dad leaves the factory at 5A and goes past the Sports Centre at 4A.

Then _____

_____

_____

_____

_____

Writing from grid references – 3

● Look at this map of a farm.

● The farmer wants to get his tractor from the shed.
What does he pass on his way from the farmhouse?

1A _____   3A _____

2B _____   4A _____

● The farmer is on his tractor. Which way does he go to get the hay?

The farmer gets his tractor from the shed at 5A. He _____

_____

_____

_____

_____

_____

Recipes – 1

This is a recipe for making your teacher sing.

Ingredients

1 quiet piano
10 quiet children

a happy song
a sunny day

Method

Place the teacher at the piano.
Children sing a happy song.
Children stop singing.
Wait five seconds.
Teacher sings a happy song.

● Now make a recipe for a good night's sleep.

Recipes – 2

This is a recipe for turning wood into gold.

Ingredients
Wood
2 gold coins
3 rusty nails
1 cup of sunshine

Method
Place in a large saucepan.
Stir seven times.
Heat over a cold fire.
Pour into six pots.
Leave to cool......

● Now make a recipe to turn stones into jelly babies.

Reporting – a fishy tale

● Write a report about what has happened in the picture.

_____

_____

_____

_____

_____

Reporting – the broken window

● Write a report about what has happened in the picture.

_____

_____

_____

_____

_____

Reporting – the cycling accident

● Write a report about what has happened in the picture.

_____

_____

_____

_____

_____

_____

Reporting – storm damage

● Write a report about what has happened in the picture.

_____

_____

_____

_____

_____

_____